Developing Sport Psychology
Within Your Clinical Practice

Jack J. Lesyk

Developing Sport Psychology Within Your Clinical Practice

A Practical Guide for Mental Health Professionals

Jossey-Bass Publishers
San Francisco

Substantial discounts on bulk quantities of Jossey-Bass books are available to corporations, professional associations, and other organizations. For details and discount information, contact the special sales department at Jossey-Bass Inc., Publishers (415) 433–1740; Fax (800) 605–2665.

For sales outside the United States, please contact your local Simon & Schuster International Office.

Jossey-Bass Web address: http://www.josseybass.com

TCF Manufactured in the United States of America using Lyons Falls D'Anthology paper, which is a special blend of non-tree fibers and totally chlorine-free wood pulp.

Library of Congress Cataloging-in-Publication Data

Lesyk, Jack J., date.
    Developing sport psychology within your clinical practice/Jack
J. Lesyk.—1st ed.
      p.   cm.
    Includes bibliographical references and index.
    ISBN 0-7879-4046-1 (alk. paper)
      1. Athletes—Mental health.   2. Athletes—Mental health services.
3. Athletes—Counseling of.   4. Sports—Psychological aspects.
I. Title.
RC451.4:A83L47 1998
616.89'0088'796—dc21   97-45764
                                                  CIP

FIRST EDITION
HC *Printing* 10 9 8 7 6 5 4 3 2 1

Contents

To my parents,
Joseph and Martha Lesyk,
who taught me

To dream "big dreams"
To pursue those dreams
To enjoy the pursuit

Preface

This book is written for experienced psychologists, social workers, psychiatrists, counselors, and other mental health professionals who are seeking to expand their practices into the new and growing area of sport psychology. Many of the techniques used in sport psychology derive from general principles of psychology and the clinical applications of behaviorism, cognitive-behavioral, and social learning theory that clinicians are already familiar with and can learn to apply within a sport psychology context.

This book provides practical guidance to clinicians seeking to build on and expand their existing skills into this new area. After a brief summary of my experiences in developing sport psychology as a major part of my practice over sixteen years, the remainder of the book is written in a progressive fashion. The early chapters encourage you to examine your personal and professional priorities and current practice in order to establish goals that include sport psychology. Then I address methods for increasing your knowledge, skills, and credentials in sport psychology so that you can expand and practice within the limits of your competence, as required by professional ethics and state law.

The subsequent chapters deal with changes in your work that are modest and only a small step from what you're already doing. In these early chapters, we explore the use of prescribed exercise as an adjunct to psychotherapy, especially in helping clients with problems associated with depression, anxiety, and self-esteem. Then we look at ways of using some new techniques with your current clinical clients, techniques that have been used successfully with athletes.

At the next level, you'll be introduced to expanding your practice to work with a new group of clients: athletes themselves, from the casual recreational athlete through the elite professional. Specific techniques are illustrated throughout the book with both brief and extended case examples. Special issues and problems of such groups as women athletes, youth in sports, and injured and aging athletes are discussed.

The book concludes with practical suggestions and guidelines for marketing your sport psychology services in a wide variety of ways. In addition to offering practical how-to-do-it information, a large collection of additional resources for your continued development are listed in the Appendix.

ACKNOWLEDGMENTS

Many people contributed directly and indirectly to the writing of this book. Special thanks are accorded to my friend Michael L. Sachs, whose interest and encouragement of my sport psychology pursuits have been appreciated for a very long time. Most recently, he was helpful in reviewing and sharing information with me on Internet resources for sport psychology. Bonnie G. Berger gave of her time and experience in helping me prepare the section on AAASP certification. Thanks to Kate F. Hays, an expert on the subject of this book herself, for telling me to "go for it" and supporting my efforts, and to Alan Rinzler, Jossey-Bass senior editor, who told me, "You can write this book," before I believed it myself.

Danny Ferry, Matt Ghaffari, and Julie Isphording—all outstanding athletes—reviewed and helped shape the section on understanding and working with elite athletes. My lifetime friend Steve Rumbaugh reviewed and offered valuable suggestions for the chapter on marketing a sport psychology practice.

Thanks to my wife, Linda, and son, Jayson, for their support and understanding when the demands of this book and its deadlines seriously encroached on family time and fun.

Many friends and clients, unnamed here for reasons of confidentiality and sheer numbers, shared their lives with me and provided me with the experiences and motivation for writing this book.

Many of the ideas expressed in this book evolved from personal contact with professional colleagues. I'd welcome and appreciate more such contact, feedback, new ideas, and sharing of experiences from readers. The best way to be in touch is by e-mail; my address is jjlesyk@sportpsych.org.

January 1998   JACK J. LESYK
Beachwood, Ohio

Growth has not only rewards and pleasures but also many intrinsic pains and always will have. Each step forward is a step into the unfamiliar and is possibly dangerous. It also means giving up something familiar and good and satisfying. It frequently means a parting and a separation, even a kind of death prior to rebirth, with consequent nostalgia, fear, loneliness and mourning. It also means giving up a simpler and easier and less effortful life, in exchange for a more demanding, more responsible, more difficult life. Growth forward *is in spite* of these losses and therefore requires courage, will, choice, and strength in the individual, as well as protection, permission, and encouragement from the environment.

ABRAHAM H. MASLOW, *Toward a Psychology of Being*

Introduction
A Long and Winding Road

You are probably reading this book because you're thinking about or have already begun to develop sport psychology within your clinical practice. You've probably also discovered that there is no single pathway to developing a sport psychology practice, just as there was no clear pathway in developing your clinical practice. In a sense, each of us has to find his own way, so this is a book about change and evolution. It's a mixture of "how I did it" and "how you can do it."

I have been engaged in the full-time private practice of clinical and sport psychology since 1983. Prior to that, I had a small, part-time practice that I began in 1979 while employed at a state psychiatric hospital. Currently approximately one-third of my client contact hours are with athletes who have sought my services for counseling related to their sport participation or are coming for mental skills training and performance enhancement. This aspect of my practice has grown considerably in the past five years and continues to increase. This recent growth can be attributed to my intense efforts to develop this aspect of my practice and to the increased acceptance, visibility, and demand for sport psychology services.

I have worked with athletes from over twenty different sports, at competitive levels ranging from scholastic to world class, Olympic, and professional. In a typical week I may have individual sessions with a ten-year-old figure skater whose precompetition anxiety is so strong that she throws up before a performance and with a twenty-five-year-old celebrity NBA basketball player who knows that mental skills training will bring him closer to performing at his full potential. In the same week I may give an evening talk to a parents' group at a local high school, conduct a one-hour small-group session in relaxation training for equestrians in my office, and meet with a local high school tennis coach and team. Working with highly motivated individuals who are goal oriented and aspiring to a high level of excellence brings me personal and professional satisfaction. I didn't get here overnight, nor was this the specific goal that I set out to achieve when I began my professional career, so let me tell you how I got here.

Personal fulfillment through my work has always been important to me. A long time ago, when I was in high school and immature in many ways, I nevertheless realized that I would spend a large portion of my life working. No one had to tell me the importance of discovering work that would be satisfying. Later I learned that Carl Rogers, Abraham Maslow, and others, such as Joseph Campbell, espoused similar viewpoints in eschewing artificial distinctions between work and play. Campbell summed up his advice in the phrase, "Follow your bliss." Today I would refine my criteria for work satisfaction and say that my goal is to do work that (1) is fun, (2) is of benefit to others, (3) enables me to earn a decent living, (4) is challenging, and (5) enables me to grow. These are my Big Five. When all are experienced, I enjoy my work and myself most fully. In a typical week, I usually have some experiences that fulfill all of these criteria. I consider myself lucky in this regard. A series of constant changes that led me to sport psychology has brought this about.

In the fall of 1962, I began graduate studies in clinical psychology at Case Western Reserve University. The department's faculty was representative of the evolution that was going on in the field of psychology. Several of my professors were Freudian, others psychodynamic, eclectic, and radical Skinnerian. George Albee, the department chair, was president of the American Psychological Association and an early advocate of a social learning, prevention approach to psychopathology, in contrast to the medical model and disease orientation that dominated the field at that time, and still does today. This point of view became the foundation of all of my subsequent clinical work, although over the years I have had to learn how to coexist with several generations of DSMs, insurance companies, and managed care organizations.

During my graduate years, I had become excited by Robert White's theory of efficacy and Julian Rotter's internal-external locus of control concepts. White hypothesized that "when action is focalized, intended, and effortful, and when it produces effects on the bit of the environment toward which it is aimed, the consequent experience includes a feeling of efficacy, a feeling of power to be an effective agent" (White, 1965, p. 203).

In my mind, White's formulation provided a common ground for understanding many of the important issues in self-esteem, self-regulation, depression, and intrinsic motivation. Years later, his words took on new meaning for me in understanding the feeling that an athlete experiences while performing well and the yearning to experience this feeling of efficacy over and over again.

About a year before completing my doctorate degree, I accepted my first professional position as a psychologist at Cleveland State Hospital, a large, overcrowded, antiquated facility. I had been hired to help establish and administer a residential token economy program for long-term, chronic schizophrenic women. My job was to work on the ward and train psychiatric aides to apply principles of contingent reinforcement to therapeutic programming for these severely regressed patients. The position also enabled me to conduct my dissertation research, a study that supported the hypothesis that not only would behavior change, but also certain cognitions as well. Indeed, my study showed a significant shift toward internal locus of control: the belief that one's actions have an effect on the environment. During this era in my life, I loved my work and experienced big doses of my Big Five on a regular basis. It is only now, many years later, in the private practice of clinical and sport psychology, that I have once again approached such joy and satisfaction in my work and in being a psychologist.

Over the next sixteen years, I remained in the state hospital system, occupying a variety of positions. The hospital where I worked, as well as the state department of mental health, was becoming increasing political, and various power struggles that ensued seriously impaired the development of effective treatment programs. For many years, I sought to experience again the satisfaction that I knew on the token economy ward, but nothing came close. The positive feelings that I sought had became fewer and fewer, and in 1983 I left the security of state employment to pursue the risky goal of transforming my small, part-time practice into a full-time livelihood.

Initially my practice was not particularly specialized. I provided a wide range of services, including individual psychotherapy for adolescents, adults, and elderly, plus counseling for couples. My clients for the most part were responsible, hard-working people who functioned fairly well from outward appearances but had serious difficulties or psychological discomfort in at least one major area of their lives. My approach, based on my earlier experiences with the most difficult of institutionalized patients, was positive, goal oriented, cognitive-behavioral, and aimed at helping people become more in control of their lives. Over time the practice grew, and I learned much about marketing and practice development, subjects that had never been taught, or even discussed, in graduate school. These learnings were most valuable when I decided to emphasize and develop the sport psychology aspect of the practice.

One area that began to develop into a specialty and greatly contributed to the growth of my practice was programs addressing health-related behavioral changes. I began offering individual and group programs in smoking cessation, weight control, and stress management. These programs brought me in contact with large numbers of people in a relatively short period of time, and word of mouth helped the practice to develop rapidly. It was also refreshing to be working with highly motivated people who had many personal, interpersonal, and financial resources available to them in addressing their goals. They responded quickly and were enthusiastic about their accomplishments and the services that I provided. I discovered that unlike those who seek a therapist for depression, anxiety, and other more traditional clinical services, those who come for positive, wellness-oriented, lifestyle changes are much more likely to talk to others and promote referrals.

Around this time several events were occurring in my life that set the stage for my early interest and involvement in sport psychology. In 1979, at the age of thirty-eight, I went through a personal transformation that was to affect my practice in a major way. At that time I had been a heavy cigarette smoker for about eighteen years. Having begun in college, like so many of my generation, I typically smoked two to three packs a day. My many attempts to quit over the previous ten years had led to failure and significant disappointment. Realizing that after age forty one begins to pay a heavy price for abusing one's body, I vowed to celebrate my fortieth birthday as a healthy, vigorous, nonsmoker, so on a beautiful April day in 1979, I stopped smoking forever and began running.

My first run lasted all of four and a half minutes. Although I thought I was going at top speed, little old ladies were walking faster and mocking me. At the end of this brief run, I was out of breath. My heart was pounding, and everything hurt. I thought I would die. Nevertheless, the next day I ran again and have continued running ever since. Two months later, I entered a five-mile race, and since then, I have been hooked on running and racing. On my fortieth birthday, I celebrated by running twenty miles. Two years after I began running, I completed my first marathon, an experience that radically changed my self-concept and my future goals. Perhaps similar to the experience of those who are transformed by walking on hot coals, I felt very profoundly that if I could quit smoking and run a marathon, I could do anything. Since then I have run 24,328 miles and completed over fourteen marathons, including New York, Chicago, and finally the Boston Marathon. Ironically in the past few years, the running that gave birth to my sport psychology practice has suffered as a result. The demands of the practice have curtailed the hours available to me for training and competing at the level of intensity that I had enjoyed in the past. Nevertheless, I try to run each morning and to compete in several races each year. One of my current personal goals is to manage my practice in such a way that will allow me to return to a higher level of running and competition in the near future.

Running transformed me as a person. I began to discover the physical and mental benefits of daily aerobic exercise and felt more energetic. I was more awake during the day and slept better at night. I was able to handle stress more effectively. So much of my life had been devoted to the development and use of my mental abilities that developing my physical capabilities was exciting.

For me, the highest level of personal transformation through running has come from competing in marathons. The marathon encompasses elements that are similar to training (the pace) and racing (the goal) but provides its own unique components. It is an endurance event, in which the distance (26.2 miles) exceeds the body's ability to store muscle glycogen (about 20 miles). Thus, no matter how well trained the marathoner, there is always "the wall": the situation when the body has depleted its stored glycogen and must switch to less efficient free-fat molecules for fuel. Experientially this is a time of agony; muscles stiffen and hurt. Whatever the pace, it feels to me as if I have suddenly gone into slow motion. As in no other race, I must dig deep into my character reserves to find the determination to continue the effort toward the finish line when every cell in my mind and body is screaming, "Stop!" Running "through the wall" and reaching the finish line, however, leads to an ecstasy that makes it worthwhile.

The secret of the marathon, if there is one, is preparation. For me, that means having a goal and a plan for achieving the goal, and following the plan religiously. My marathon training plan consists of three months of daily runs, each planned in advance (based on expert advice) with regard to distance, pace, and purpose. Most marathoners will tell you that finishing their first marathon was a transforming event in their lives. After finishing my first in 1981, I felt a renewed self-confidence that would generalize to other areas of my life. From that experience, I found the strength to leave the safety and security of hospital employment and assume the risks of private practice. I found the courage to end a dysfunctional marriage. I came to believe that major goals are accomplished by daring to have big dreams and by translating those dreams into a plan that specifies small, daily steps that will lead to that goal. Or as others have said, "How do you eat an elephant?" The same way you eat a hamburger (or anything)—one bite at a time.

Through my immersion in running and working with athletes, I discovered for myself what others have written about: sport is a metaphor for life. In sports and in life, there are goals, limited resources, obstacles, rules, penalties, and outcomes. Part of the appeal of sports, for both athletes and spectators, is that in sports each of these elements is relatively simple, clear, easily understood, and slowly changing. In the rest of life, by contrast, these elements are usually complex and ever changing, often at a confusing and rapid rate. At the end of a hard day at the office, there is no clear measure of outcome or of how well I've performed. At the end of a race, my finishing time tells me exactly how well I've done.

Sport as a metaphor for life is easily understood and useful. I have introduced this way of thinking to clients in my clinical practice, as well as in consulting with business groups and in presenting stress management seminars. Surprisingly, few people that I've encountered have analyzed their life situations and problems in terms of goals, limited resources, obstacles, rules, penalties, and outcomes. Once introduced to this model, most clients come to accept it enthusiastically and benefit by its use.

As you might surmise, running competitively stimulated my interest in the mental aspects of running as well as other sports. Introspectively, I thought about the issues of setting goals, maintaining commitment and enthusiasm for a training plan, managing the night-before-a-marathon anxieties, maintaining focus and following my game plan during a race, running through pain and discomfort, dealing with disappointment, and maintaining balance in my life. When I turned to my discipline of psychology for answers, I discovered that very little had been published. I read the few available books by Terry Orlick, Robert Nideffer, Dorothy Harris, and Richard Suinn, and what I learned was useful to me as an athlete and a psychologist. It confirmed and validated many of my own beliefs and introduced me to new concepts and techniques. Most of all, it inspired me to picture myself working with other athletes, helping them to understand and improve the mental aspects of their sport.

A second influence that prepared me for my entry into sport psychology was my interest and learning in hypnosis and mental imagery. After I quit smoking and began developing smoking cessation programs, I became aware of the positive use of hypnosis in such programs and began to read widely on this topic. I took an intensive training workshop with T. X. Barber, as well as several other related workshops. The topic was fascinating and useful in my practice, as well as in my running and personal life. I began to realize how much I had intuitively used mental imagery and mental rehearsal as far back in my own life as I could remember. Now, with training, I would be able to use these techniques in a more focused and intensive manner, both personally and professionally. Once again I had experienced the thrill of learning and venturing into new territory.

My professional entrance into sport psychology occurred unexpectedly on a rainy October afternoon in 1981. A highly distraught mother of a sixteen-year-old figure skater needed help for her son.

Matt, as it turned out, was a national-level competitor. After several years of considerable success, however, his recent competitions had not gone well, and instead of excitement before competition, he was experiencing extreme dread and anxiety. Could I help? I saw Matt the next day and began meeting with him weekly for several months. After gathering additional information about Matt's history and the circumstances of his recent competitions, I viewed his competition anxiety as similar to a clinical phobia and began working with him from that perspective. First, I began to teach Matt how to relax his body through the use of progressive relaxation, a technique adapted from Edmund Jacobson. Our session was recorded on audiotape, so Matt could practice relaxation at home on a daily basis. Two weeks later, I instructed him in mental relaxation using light hypnosis, also recorded for home practice.

Within a few weeks, Matt learned to assess his own level of relaxation and was beginning to induce relaxation, through cue words in real-life situations, without using the tape. Next, I asked him to describe his skating program step by step, so that I could construct a mental imagery rehearsal script. Later, while he was in a relaxed state, I guided his mental images through a successful performance of his program. Again, I recorded this material for his home practice. Additionally, we discussed the types of self-talk and images that he typically experienced just prior to major competition. Together we created a more positive set of statements and images that would better prepare Matt for difficult competition. Within a few months, Matt began skating much better in competition and was enjoying himself as well. We continued our work on an as-needed basis for about a year. After considerable success in amateur competition, Matt retired a few years later to begin a career with Ice Capades. About ten years later, he returned home to become a figure skater teacher. We've come full circle, and now he occasionally calls to refer one of his students who's in near panic before a major competition.

Through Matt, I got to know his coach, and she referred other students to me. Thus began my relationship with the figure skating community in my geographic area, a valued relationship that I have nurtured ever since.

After working with Matt and a few other skaters, I was eager to continue with more athletes but realized that I had to be more assertive if I wanted to expand the sport psychology aspect of my practice. The following summer I attended a one-week running camp on the campus of Ohio University in Athens. Each day consisted of a morning and evening run, two lectures on some aspect of running, and much camaraderie. One afternoon a professor of exercise physiology gave an hour-long talk on the mental aspects of running. He began with a memorized, eloquent recitation of "Casey at Bat" and an apology for not knowing much about the topic about which he was going to speak! Afterward I spoke with him and discussed sport psychology and my experiences. He graciously invited me to give the talk the following summer, an invitation that I was pleased to accept. Becoming affiliated with the Distance Runners Camp at Ohio University provided me with exposure and credibility among serious runners and their coaches. Later this visibility enabled me to write a column on the mental aspects of running in the *Ohio Runner* magazine and develop a referral base in the community of serious, competitive runners.

Although I continued my self-education in sport psychology by reading the limited published materials that were available, most of my applied work involved translating established clinical psychology techniques to the special needs of athletes. Although this seemed appropriate to me, I believed that I needed to validate this perspective and receive additional training from those with more experience working with athletes.

A pivotal opportunity presented itself when I received an announcement for the U.S. Olympic Committee's first conference on sport psychology to be held in Long Beach, California, the following September. The conference, entitled "Sports Psychology 1984: A Scientific Approach to High Performance," was all that I had hoped it would be. The presenters were the all-stars of the sport psychology world—those who had written the books I had relied so heavily on, including Bruce Ogilvie, Dorothy Harris, Richard Suinn, Robert Nideffer, Rainer Martens, Denis Waitley, Betty Wenz, Jerry May, and William Morgan. Fewer than a hundred attended that two-day conference, so there was close, intimate contact with the presenters, who were approachable and helpful. I returned to Cleveland inspired, motivated, and with the belief that my self-education and application of psychology principles to athletes was consistent with the work of the experts. I also learned new techniques for assessment and performance-enhancement interventions.

Over the next four or five years, the sport psychology aspect of my practice developed, though rather slowly. By around 1990, I began to receive more referrals from sources I had cultivated over the years. Around this time I began conducting intensive, small-group mental skills training workshops for specific sports. These well-received workshops increased the visibility of my work in sport psychology and generated favorable newspaper publicity and referrals. In addition, the positive media attention to sport psychology during the Olympics and occasional articles on professional athletes who used sport psychologists encouraged further growth and development.

Another change was the increased numbers of junior and senior high school athletes who were requesting my services. Only a few years before, these younger athletes seemed to fear a stigma if it were known that they were seeing a "shrink." As illustrated by patterns of use of high tech athletic equipment, nutritional concepts, and training techniques, elite athletes are the first to access new technology; then there is a "trickle down" to progressively lower levels of competition. So now sport psychology was beginning to trickle down with the positive endorsement of celebrity athletes, and I was in an excellent position to respond to the need. I captured this concept in the advertising slogan, "Most serious athletes need a sport psychologist. Until now, only elite athletes have been able to have one."

Until 1993, I marketed my practice as "Jack J. Lesyk, Ph.D., Inc., Clinical and Sport Psychology." History and habit made it difficult for me to present myself otherwise. I worried that if my visibility became too linked to sport psychology, my clinical practice and reputation would suffer. Gradually I began to realize that although I viewed my practice as one entity, in fact, it served two distinctly different populations and that my efforts to promote a combined practice were diluting the effectiveness of my efforts and serving neither well.

Consequently I established the Ohio Center for Sport Psychology. Although the center would initially be the sport psychology part of my private practice, my concept was that the center would offer a wider range of services than I had as an individual and that these services would be provided by a wide range of professionals. Both of these objectives have been partially fulfilled.

As I look back at the twenty-eight years that have passed since the completion of my graduate work, I have appreciated and enjoyed a wide variety of settings and individuals in my work. I am amazed at times that my professional work has allowed me to experience and share in the lives of backward, regressed, schizophrenic patients, extremely successful professional members of my community, and celebrity Olympic and professional athletes. I feel a personal richness from my work and am struck by the commonality, rather than the divergence, of these clients. My role in each of their lives has been to help them reduce suffering, increase their enjoyment of life, and develop more effective ways of reaching their goals. In this day of specific treatments for specific disorders, I continue to treasure the broad-based nature of my graduate training in the general principles of psychology and clinical psychology. This broad base has enabled me to adapt and adjust to the changing times and changing needs for psychological services.

You've now read the "How I Did It" part of this book. Now let's begin to see "How You Can Do It, Too."

Reference

White, R. W. (1965). The experience of efficacy in schizophrenia. *Psychiatry, 28,* 199–211.

Developing Sport Psychology Within Your Clinical Practice

Setting the Course for Change
Analysis, Planning, and New Opportunities

W hat has stimulated your interest in developing sport psychology within your clinical practice? Perhaps you've discovered the positive effects of physical exercise on your own health, mood, and thinking. Perhaps you are a serious competitive athlete and have acquired firsthand knowledge about the mental aspects of sport. Perhaps you've become aware of the increasing visibility of sport psychology in the media. Maybe you've become disillusioned with insurance companies, managed care, or competition from other clinicians and are looking for a new niche for your practice in the marketplace. Or maybe you just need a change for change's sake, with new goals, new techniques, and more clients. You may have already ventured into this arena and wish to develop it in a more systematic fashion.

Change is inevitable. Even if we don't change, the people and circumstances around us do, and we still experience the consequences. If we are passive and forfeit our influence in the process, we may come to feel ourselves as victims of the change. Often a client will say, "But it's so difficult to change." My response, "Yes, but have you thought about how difficult it is to not change?"

Change is costly in terms of time, energy, risk, disruption, and effort without immediate reward. To ensure that your sacrifices will result in the benefits that will make these disruptions and risks worthwhile, you must engage in analysis and planning rather than dealing with change in a haphazard, piecemeal, impulsive manner.

The planning process begins with self-reflection on your reasons for wanting to change. What discomforts do you want to eliminate or reduce, and what growth and development experiences do you hope to experience? What is the nature of your practice now? How would you like it to be at some specified point in the future? What's the plan for getting there? What resources do you already have, and what additional ones do you need? Are you sufficiently committed to your plan? With these points in mind, let's take a look at your practice.

YOUR REASONS FOR CHANGE

When I begin working with an athlete, I want to know why he participates in his sport and what benefits he expects from that participation. I also want to know the degree to which his expected benefits are actually being experienced. Thus, I have devised a questionnaire, the Mental Skills Assessment Form (see the Appendix), on which the athlete selects his five most important reasons for sport participation from a list of fifteen commonly stated reasons (for example, earning respect from other people, having fun, learning life skills, and financial gains). Next, he is asked to indicate the extent to which he is currently experiencing satisfaction in each of his chosen areas (on a scale of 1 to 5, "not at all" to "a great deal"). This information enables me to evaluate the need and direction for intervention. Later, the same tool enables me to evaluate the personal impact of any changes that have occurred.

The same questions are relevant in assessing your clinical practice and your potential for change. Let's try it. On a blank sheet of paper, list the five most important benefits that you expect to experience through your practice, in order of importance. After each one, write a number from one to five, describing the degree to which the need is currently (or typically) being fulfilled. If you have all fives, you're probably quite satisfied and have little reason for change. Any item with a score below five represents an area for potential change. Which of your practice needs are least fulfilled? Which are most fulfilled? Wherever we go from here, your planning should focus on changes that will increase the satisfaction of your specific needs that are not being currently met. The next few planning stages are intended to help you look more concretely at your current practice in this light.

YOUR PRACTICE NOW

Before exploring the many ways in which you can develop sport psychology within your clinical practice, reflect on your practice as it is right now. Imagine your office and yourself in that office. What immediate impression comes to mind? Is it predominantly favorable or unfavorable?

Location and Physical Setting

How do you feel about the location of your office? The immediate neighborhood? The building you occupy? The particular suite? Your waiting room? Your consulting room? Do you share space with others? How do you feel about them? What aspects of your location and facility do you like the most? The least? Which aspects of your physical setting make you feel the most comfortable and most productive? Which aspects interfere with your comfort and productivity?

Go through this list of questions again, this time from the point of view of the general public and of a client coming to see you for the first time. What impression do all of these create in the mind of someone who has not yet met you? What kind of mental picture would the person have of you? What expectations would he or she have of you based on that impression? Are these the images and expectations that you would want the person to have?

Go through this list yet a third time. This time, think of the impact of the location and physical setting on the financial aspects of your practice. For example, when I moved my office closer to an interstate highway, I began receiving referrals from greater distances. Does your location support the image that you want the public to have of you? Does your address suggest unusually high fees or discounted prices? Are your office artwork, furniture, and decor supportive of the image you want to you project? Which of these factors seem justified to you in terms of contributing to the financial profitability of your practice? Which factors may be a financial liability?

Clients and Services

Who are your clients? What types of clients do you enjoy working with the most? The least? What types of clients do you believe you are most effective with? The least effective? What types of problems or issues are you the most effective with? The least effective? What types of clients and issues do you want to work with more within your practice? Less of? Are there types of clients and issues that you've never worked with before but would like to?

Referral Sources

How do clients become aware of your services? What makes them decide to come to you rather than to another clinician? Who refers clients to you? Why did they first refer clients to you? Why do they continue to refer to you? Who has stopped referring clients to you? Why have they stopped referring clients to you? Whom would you like to start referring to you? What do you need to do in order to make that happen?

Treatment Modalities

What modalities of treatment do you enjoy practicing the most? Individual psychotherapy, couples and family, groups, seminars, or others? The least? Where are you the most effective? The least effective? What new modalities would you like to practice? What proportion of your time would you like to spend practicing each modality?

Professional Activities

What portion of your professional time is spent in direct client services, teaching, continuing education, practice marketing and development, report writing, dealing with insurance and managed care companies, participation in professional organizations, consultation with colleagues, research, supervision of students, writing for publication? Overall, what aspects are most enjoyable? Least enjoyable? Which activities do you want to do more of? Less of?

Financial Issues

Which aspects of your practice are most financial rewarding? Least rewarding? Overall, what is the financial health of your practice? If you keep doing what you've done in the past, what will your financial position be in five years? Ten years? What changes do you need to make in order to improve your financial position? What changes do you need to make in order to adjust to the ongoing changes in the health care industry?

Personal Balance

How much of your time and effort are devoted to your practice? To what extent does your practice support your preferred lifestyle? To what extent does it interfere? Are you satisfied with the hours you work and the quantity and scheduling of time off and vacations? To what extent is your practice a "job" versus an extension and expression of yourself?

YOUR PRACTICE IN THE FUTURE

Now peek into your future as you'd like it to be. Imagine your office and yourself in that office at some specified time in the future. What comes to mind? Go through the items in the previous section, imagining each of them the way you would like it to be. How do the scenarios of your existing and future practices compare? I hope that there are many similarities, constants that require no change and give you the secure foundation on which change can be launched. But take a close look at each of the scenarios. What differences are there between them? These contrasts can become the basis for goal setting and planning.

Now take the time to distill and extrapolate specific goals for the future development of your practice—perhaps spending more time providing educational rather than clinical services; consulting outside your office, with increased travel as part of your professional activities; or maintaining your income level but shifting your working hours so you can have more time with your family and friends. Keep a list of these goals, and make a commitment to yourself to review your progress on a regular, scheduled basis. If you have a clear set of practice goals, it will be easier for you to explore the particular ways in which you can develop sport psychology within your changing practice in a significant, planned manner.

SPORT PSYCHOLOGY OPPORTUNITIES

There are a wide variety of potential clients and services that may be considered under the broad umbrella of sport psychology. Because you are a practicing clinician, you already have a good knowledge of the basic principles of general psychology, for example, human development, sensation and perception, learning theory, motivation, personality, social psychology, and so on. The principles derived from these content areas constitute the common foundation on which clinical psychology, sport psychology, and all other applied psychology disciplines are based. Thus you're not starting from ground zero. You already have experience in applying the broad principles of psychology to specific people with specific problems and issues. In the remainder of this chapter we'll take a look at some of the broad categories of sport psychology services. Some of these will be quite close to what you're doing now, such as doing psychotherapy with athletes. Other activities, like performance enhancement, may require increasing your knowledge and skills.

Using Sport Psychology with Your Current Clients

A modest beginning to using appropriate concepts and techniques of sport and exercise psychology in working with your regular clinical clients involves a conceptual shift rather than a major redefinition of your practice, clients, or modalities. This shift moves you and your clients away from a reactive, medical model, pathology-oriented paradigm and toward a positive, health-oriented way of thinking. It acknowledges the connection of mental health to exercise and physical activity. It also requires some basic understanding of sport psychology, the topic of the next chapter.

As you begin to develop sport psychology within your clinical practice, you will find that prescribed exercise is an excellent adjunct to psychotherapy in treating your usual clients with anxiety disorders, depression, self-esteem, and many other issues. At this stage in your development, you work with your usual client population and improve your psychotherapeutic effectiveness by adding new conceptual and practical techniques to your professional repertoire. For example, Marsha, a fifty-two-year-old, recently widowed accountant with a long history of mild depression, experienced clinical improvement after committing herself to a daily brisk walk in addition to psychotherapy.

Clinical Sport Psychology

In 1983, the U.S. Olympic Committee's Advisory Board on sport psychology defined three types of sport psychology specializations: research, clinical, and education. While the development of research in sport psychology lies outside the scope of this book, the other two specializations have direct implications for the development of your practice.

Clinical sport psychology is essentially the application of professional clinical services to athletes. Obviously athletes are subject to the same psychological and psychiatric disorders that are experienced by any other population: disorders related to adjustment, mood, anxiety, eating, sleep, substance abuse, sexual issues, and so forth. They are affected as well by issues associated with relationships, self-confidence, finances, health and injuries, emotional control, communications, time management, decision making, and setting goals and priorities. The disorders and issues that you are most experienced and knowledgeable about are good areas in which to begin working with athletes, as an expansion of your current practice. In fact, the concept "athlete" is far too broad to be very useful, so you might wish to consider specific athlete subpopulations that you are planning to work with, such as adolescent figure skaters, middle-aged golfers, marathon runners, or major league professional players. In thinking about delivering your clinical services to the athletic community, consider as well coaches, athletic directors, parents and spouses of athletes, and referees, all of whom also have clinical needs.

As with any other client population that you begin working with, it is essential to learn about the subculture. In what ways are athletes similar to the clients you're now working with? In what ways are they different?

If you are a serious participant in a sport yourself, that might be a good place to start. As you develop your clinical practice in this direction, you may see yourself as primarily applying your traditional clinical skills, but you will come to be regarded as "someone who really understands _____ [equestrians, basketball players, or the sport of your choice]." Bob, for example, was a forty-one-year-old high school basketball coach who came to me for stress management. After several highly successful seasons, his team was halfway through the worst season in the school's history. Blaming himself and losing perspective, Bob was having difficulty sleeping, was quite irritable, and had trouble concentrating while teaching his classes. Although his team performance did not improve that season, Bob benefited from cognitive behavioral therapy and made a better adjustment to the situation. About six years later, he returned to therapy with me when he became burned out with coaching and needed help to retire and find new interests.

Educational Sport Psychology

This subdiscipline may represent a departure from your formal training and everyday work as a clinician. In this specialty, you need to acquire expertise in assessing and teaching the mental skills necessary for high-level sport performance. You'll be working with athletes who may be relatively free of diagnosable psychiatric and psychological disorders, who may be very well adjusted, and who have a strong drive to perform up to their potential. Some will come to you because of disappointment in a recent performance, perhaps because of anxiety or attention control problems. Others come without a specific problem. They are performing very well but know that they are capable of even better performances, if they can improve their mental skills.

The format and venue for these educational services may vary considerably more than with traditional clinical services. On occasion you may work intensively one-on-one with these athletes in your office. At other times, you may observe and work with them in their actual sports environment—the skating rink, the football field, or the swimming pool. Or you may review videotapes of their recent performances in competition or training. When beneficial, you may meet with their coaches (with their permission, of course).

Other educational services may be delivered within a group format, either as a one-shot presentation or as part of a series of sessions. Over the past year, for example, I have made the following presentations:

A one-hour lecture in a local high school auditorium to forty high school coaches on how to help young athletes get the most benefit from their sport participation

A four-hour mental skills training workshop in a local hotel conference center for sixty adult equestrians

A six-week mental skills training workshop in my office conference room for seven tennis players, held for one hour once a week

A one-hour presentation in a school meeting room to parents of young athletes on how to be emotionally supportive of their children

The mental skills associated with high-level performance, especially under pressure, are often referred to as performance-enhancement techniques. Teaching these skills to individual athletes or groups of athletes is collectively referred to as psychological skills training or mental skills training. These specific skills, derived from principles of general psychology, clinical psychology, and psychology of stress management, have been well developed in the sport psychology literature, and it would be wise for the newcomer to become familiar with that literature. Specific suggestions for accomplishing that will be offered in the next chapter. The skills that are generally enumerated in this area include:

- *Motivation.*   Successful elite athletes are aware of the benefits that they expect to experience through sport participation. They have the ability to persist through difficult tasks and difficult times, even when these benefits are not immediately forthcoming.

- *Setting and achieving goals.*   Successful elite athletes set long-term and short-term goals that are realistic, behavioral, measurable, and time oriented. They can assess their performance level, develop a specific, detailed plan for attaining their goals, and identify and obtain the resources necessary to achieve those goals.

- *Arousal control.*   Successful elite athletes can discover and regulate their optimal state of emotional arousal prior to and during competition.

- *Attention control.*   Successful elite athletes have the ability to develop a precise awareness of what stimuli they need to attend to during a particular game or sport situation. They can maintain focus on these stimuli and resist distraction, whether from the environment or from within themselves; regain focus when it has been lost during competition; and play in the here-and-now without regard to either past or anticipated future events.

• *Self-talk.* Successful elite athletes manage their self-confidence and challenges in a positive, constructive manner through healthy habits of self-talk. Sometimes self-talk is based on cognitive-behavioral strategies for reframing a situation, or sometimes it is simply a cue word selected to elicit specific thoughts, feelings, and behaviors.

• *Emotional control.* Successful elite athletes can control strong emotions, such as anger, elation, or despondency, to prevent them from interfering with performance. These emotional states frequently accompany mistakes and errors, or sometimes even performing above one's expectations.

• *Mental imagery.* Successful elite athletes can imagine themselves performing specific behaviors at a high level of excellence clearly and vividly, using multiple sensory modalities. They can mentally rehearse situations and performances and deal with errors and poor performances through mental imagery correction rather than reliving the mistake mentally.

These mental skills are associated not only with successful performance in sport but in other many other areas of life as well, such as school, business, or developing a successful professional practice. This commonality provides a good linkage between your sport psychology activities and using this model with other clinical and nonclinical clients.

Team Consultation

Often sport psychologists affiliated with teams are essentially teaching performance-enhancement techniques to members of the team on an individual or group basis. At other times, they may be asked to "bring the team together" or provide "team-building" services. This specialty requires knowledge in such areas as group dynamics, leadership psychology, communication, and team-building techniques. During the past year, for example, I've met on a regular basis with a local high school tennis team to help the players maintain a feeling of cohesion during the off-season, as well as to teach mental skills. Several years ago, I was contracted on an emergency basis to help resolve serious differences between a college soccer team and the coach. In a letter to the athletic director, all of the players threatened to resign from the team unless the coach was removed for reasons of verbal abuse. My intervention temporarily ameliorated the situation until the coach resigned a year later.

Professional Requirements

The professional practicing clinical sport psychology is required to be licensed in order to diagnose and treat mental and emotional disorders. Educational sport psychology activities have no such stringent requirement. In fact, for years, coaches, teachers, athletic trainers, and fellow athletes have, for better or for worse, taught these mental skills to others. Within the domain of contemporary sport psychology, there are individuals whose professional training has been in psychology and others who come from physical education backgrounds. Although the debate continues as to what is the most appropriate training for those who practice sport psychology, the reality is that individuals from both academic backgrounds currently practice educational sport psychology activities as described in this section. Those without a license in psychology are restricted from using the title "psychologist" in presenting themselves to the public.

Regardless of one's professional background, all mental health professionals are required by ethics and by law to practice within their scope of their proficiency. For example, in Ohio, the psychology licensing law states that a psychologist shall limit his or her practice "to those specialty areas in which competence has been gained through education, training, and experience."

Now that you've taken a close look at your practice and established goals for yourself, your next step will be to discover a pathway that will take you to your goals. Chapter Two is devoted to an important aspect of that pathway: developing your knowledge, skills, and credentials in sport psychology.

2

Developing Your Knowledge, Skills, and Credentials in Sport Psychology

Like many of us, you probably completed your graduate or professional training long before you heard of universities offering courses or degrees in sport psychology. You're busy managing your practice and trying to balance your personal life as well. So it is unlikely that you're going to close your practice, go back to a university, and earn a degree in sport psychology. An important part of your professional training was learning to learn so that you'd be able to continue your development through self-directed educational experiences throughout your career. By now, you've no doubt already experienced significant development beyond your formal training in other areas of specialization through reading, discussion with colleagues, and attending seminars and conferences. These same modalities are available to you as you begin to integrate sport psychology into your clinical practice.

In this chapter I've identified and enumerated resources that will help you to access essential information quickly and easily. Fortunately, these days there is an abundance of such resources.

YOUR OWN SPORTS EXPERIENCE

Your own sports participation is not a formal prerequisite for practicing sport psychology, but in truth I've never met a sport psychologist who did not have a history of sports participation at some level. Most, in fact, regardless of age and gender, are currently engaged in some form of sport activity. Your own sport experience, then, is a good point of departure for your journey into this new area of practice. Consider your own experience:

- What have you learned about the mental aspects of sport through your own experience?

- How have you dealt with the issues of motivation, setting and achieving goals, controlling your arousal, relaxation, concentration, and emotions?

- What have you learned about mental imagery and the effects of self-talk?

- Do you know of friends, competitors, or serious athletes in this sport who seem to have a good mental game? What are their techniques? How did they acquire them?

- Have you improved your mental game? If so, how did you accomplish this?

- What mental goals do you have for yourself? How will you attain these goals? What resources do you need?

After thinking about the mental aspects of your sport, what you've learned, and what you'd like to learn, determine how representative your sport is of all sports. There are some common denominators, yet each sport is unique as well. What have you learned from your sport experience that can be generalized to all or almost all athletes? To which specific sports are your experiences partially relevant? To which sports are your experiences mostly limited?

If you haven't done so already, an excellent way of beginning to practice sport psychology is to practice on yourself. Besides being a learning method that will give you firsthand knowledge and personal conviction, you're also most unlikely to get reported to your licensing board for practicing beyond your areas of demonstrated competence. Whatever your sport, you may be able to find a book on improving your mental skills written specifically for that sport. This is especially true for some of the more common sports that large numbers of adults participate in, such as golf, tennis, and running. Additionally, there are excellent practical mental skills training books that are not sport specific and can be applied to virtually any sport. Both types of books are found in the Selected Readings in Sport Psychology list included in the Appendix.

READING

Perhaps the quickest way to get an overview of the field of sport psychology, as well as to acquire practical information that can be applied to athlete clients, is to engage in selective reading. In addition to the books listed in the Appendix, several journals are especially relevant to applied sport psychology:

• *Journal of Applied Sport Psychology*, founded in 1989. The official publication of the Association for the Advancement of Applied Sport Psychology (AAASP), subscription is included with membership. This journal publishes articles on applied research as well as professional practice.

• *Journal of Sport and Exercise Psychology*, founded in 1979. This is the official publication of the North American Society for the Psychology of Sport and Physical Activity (NASPSPA). Published by Human Kinetics Publishers, P.O. Box 5076, Champaign, Illinois 61825–5076. In addition to basic and applied research articles, this journal contains book reviews and a regular feature, the "Sport Psychologist's Digest," a collection of short, useful summaries of articles appearing in other journals.

- *The Sport Psychologist*, founded in 1987. Also published by Human Kinetics Publishers. In addition to applied research, this journal publishes articles pertinent to professional practice issues. It is also a good source of book reviews. The "Bulletin Board," which appears in each issue, provides useful news information, announcements of upcoming events and conferences, as well as availability of new books and other resources in sport psychology. Recently this journal reaffirmed its commitment to issues of practice development by creating a new position on its staff: professional practice editor.

PROFESSIONAL ORGANIZATIONS

Joining one or more of the professional organizations whose principal focus is sport psychology will provide you access to newsletters, journals, workshops, and conferences to facilitate your self-study. Besides being an effective way to receive information about the field, joining demonstrates your interest in and commitment to the field of sport psychology, an important part of establishing your credentials. Through these organizations and their publications and conferences, you will be able to stay abreast of current (and sometimes controversial) positions regarding ethics, credentials, accreditation, research, and applied techniques. The general public's awareness of sport psychology and its availability is often the result of the contributions of these organizations.

Following are the principal organizations:

- *American Psychological Association, Division 47, Sport and Exercise Psychology.*   Founded in 1987. Addresses research, practice, and professional issues in sport psychology. The division publishes a newsletter and meets annually at the time of the APA convention, usually in August. Membership information: Shertina Mack, APA Division Services. Phone: (202) 336–6013 (direct line), (800) 374–2721 (APA general line); e-mail: saj.apa@email.apa.org.

- *Association for the Advancement of Applied Sport Psychology (AAASP).* Founded in 1985. A multidisciplinary organization devoted to research and application of applied sport psychology. It is organized into three topical subareas: health psychology, intervention-performance enhancement, and social psychology. The organization holds its annual meeting in September or October. Membership information: Vikki Krane, Ph.D., AAASP Secretary-Treasurer, Bowling Green State University, School of HPER, Eppler Center, Bowling Green, Ohio 43403. Phone: (419) 372-7233; e-mail: vkrane@trapper.gbsu.edu.

- *North American Society for the Psychology of Sport and Physical Activity (NASPSPA).* Founded in 1967. Focuses its interests on research in the areas of motor learning and control, motor development, and sport and exercise psychology. It publishes the newsletter *Sport Psychology Bulletin* and holds an annual conference, usually in June. Membership information: Kathleen Williams, Secretary/Treasurer, NASPSPA, Department of Exercise and Sport Science, University of North Carolina at Greensboro, Greensboro, North Carolina 27412-5001. E-mail: WILLIAMK@iris.uncg.edu.

- *International Society of Sport Psychology (ISSP).* Founded in 1965. Predominantly a research organization that publishes the *International Journal of Sport Psychology.* The organization holds a conference every four years, usually in the summer. Membership information: Dr. Dieter Hackfort, Treasurer ISSP, ISWS der Uni BwM, Werner-Heisenberg Weg 39, D-85577 Neubiberg, Germany.

- *International Society for Sport Psychiatry (ISSP).* Founded in 1992. ISSP membership is open to psychiatrists and psychiatrists in training with an interest in sport psychiatry, and to nonpsychiatrists who have distinguished themselves in the field. The society holds an annual conference in conjunction with the meeting of the American Psychiatric Association. Membership information: Daniel

Begel, M.D., President, 316 North Milwaukee Street, Suite 318, Milwaukee, Wisconsin 53202. Phone: (414) 271–2900.

CONFERENCES, WORKSHOPS, AND SEMINARS

Attending a conference sponsored by one of the organizations listed can strengthen your understanding of sport psychology in many formal, as well as informal, ways. In addition to presentations and symposia, informal contact with other professionals with interests similar to your own can be uplifting and beneficial. Both APA, Division 47, and AAASP have intensive preconference, continuing-education workshops and seminars that often deal with the development of professional skills and practice development. Attending these conferences and earning continuing-education credits will be helpful in establishing your credentials and qualifications.

I have had particularly positive experiences attending AAASP conferences. I value the diversity of the AAASP membership—almost equal numbers of professionals from sport sciences and psychology backgrounds—and have enjoyed meeting students, as well as other clinical professionals, including those from social work and psychiatry. There is a warm, informal ambience at AAASP meetings, and I have found most members helpful, approachable, and willing to share their experiences and resources. In recent years, I have enjoyed the company of a small cadre of private practitioners, like myself, who meet each year at the conference and spend considerable time sharing and helping one another in the development of our sport psychology practices. We also maintain contact with one another between the annual conferences through writing, telephone, and e-mail.

Periodically universities and other organizations conduct workshops and seminars. These are often announced in the journals and newsletters of the organizations listed above. If you purchase sport psychology books by mail, subscribe to one of the journals, or join one of the organizations, you'll soon find yourself on the mailing list for conferences as well as other sport psychology products.

In addition to workshops and seminars promoted within the domain of sport psychology, workshops and seminars offered by a wide variety of educational and professional organizations may be of value to you in expanding your knowledge. Depending on your interests, needs, and background, you may benefit by increasing your knowledge in such areas as stress management, imagery, psychological aspects of injury and recovery, and eating disorders.

PROFESSIONAL CONTACTS

Although reading books and journals and attending the occasional conference will be invaluable in your acquisition of knowledge and skills in sport psychology, these experiences will probably not be totally sufficient. There is no substitute for regular professional interaction, on either a mentoring or collegial level. Such contact provides stimulation, cross-fertilization of ideas, feedback, and sharing of experiences.

Mentoring

If sport psychology and its content areas are a substantial departure from your professional education and experience, consider developing a mentoring relationship with someone recognized in the field. The AAASP membership directory, as well as the directories of your state and local professional associations, might be helpful in locating such a person. To ascertain whether a person is qualified to mentor you, consider some of the questions that Betty Wenz and Vincent Granito, Jr., suggest in *Consumer's Guide to Sport Psychology* (see the Appendix) for a consumer selecting a sport psychologist. A person who is an AAASP Certified Consultant or listed on the U.S. Olympic Committee's Sport Psychology Registry has met a high set of standards. However, there are other well-qualified individuals who may not appear on these lists for a variety of reasons.

Since a mentor is likely to be a high-level professional, expect to pay for the time you spend with the person. I suggest setting out a contract specifying your learning objectives, the method of helping you achieve your objectives, the frequency of meetings, the duration of contact, and agreement on fees.

Another alternative is to find a mentor who is interested in conducting a group mentoring experience for you and several other clinicians with similar learning needs. The group modality could be intellectually stimulating as well as efficient in terms of time and expense.

Collegial Study Groups

If you have a solid professional education and experience in concepts and applications close to that of sport psychology, you may not need as intense an experience as mentoring. Or you may not be able to obtain a qualified professional in your area who is willing and able to mentor. Another alternative is to form a study group of clinicians like yourself who share an interest in developing their knowledge and skills in sport psychology. Such a group would meet on a regular basis, establish learning objectives, and share reading, discussion, presentations, and case studies with one another. On occasion, the group might contract an experienced, well-qualified sport psychologist to consult with on special topics or to review or present case studies.

Individual Contacts

If a mentor or study group is unnecessary or impossible to arrange, you may wish to develop a list of qualified sport psychologists whom you can call on an as-needed basis. Several times over the years, as I was preparing to develop sport-specific workshops, I contacted well-known sport psychologists who had considerable experience with these particular sport populations. I was, in most cases, pleasantly surprised at their returning my telephone calls and their willingness to share their experiences and advice. Mindful of the importance of their time, I had done considerable preparation before contacting them and had tentative ideas and plans to present to them for their feedback and suggestions.

Since these early days, I have gotten to know a large number of sport psychologists, mostly through the AAASP meetings, and have a long list of experts whose thoughts I can solicit when I need help with a project or a difficult case. These expert resources are essential for a private practitioner, like myself, who rarely has face-to-face contact with other sport psychologists because of the inherent isolation of private practice and the relatively few numbers of sport psychologists in most locations.

THE INTERNET

No matter where you live, no matter how isolated you may be geographically from sport psychology colleagues, you can now become a regular, participating member of that community through the Internet. This medium has enabled me to maintain daily contact with sport psychology colleagues and to continue my informal professional education and development.

If you haven't discovered this electronic world yet, all you need is a computer with a modem and a service provider to connect you to the Internet. Learning how to use the Internet is relatively easy. A half-hour instruction from a friend or colleague or a self-instruction book is enough to get you started. From there, you can learn on your own, through exploration and trial and error. Although the Internet has many components and uses, here are a few that I have found to be particularly helpful.

Electronic Mail

Through e-mail I am able to reach out to individuals all over the world. Last year, for example, a colleague who lives over five hundred miles away and I planned and conducted a six-hour continuing-education workshop on the private practice of sport psychology at the AAASP meeting. During the several months prior to the conference, we communicated almost daily by e-mail, developing the proposal and the details of our presentations. Since the conference, several of the participants have contacted me by e-mail to continue discussing ideas stimulated by the workshop.

The Sportpsy Mail List

The Sportpsy list is a valuable and exciting communications tool for maintaining contact with the sport psychology community. (Instructions for subscribing to the list are given in the Appendix.) By posting an e-mail to this list, your message is automatically sent to approximately one thousand list subscribers—sport psychologists, students, athletes, coaches, parents of athletes, and others— throughout the world. Postings include requests for help on a specific topic and serious discussions of ethical issues, case problems, and philosophy.

Many users are somewhat shy at first and simply read the list messages without actively posting. For me, the greatest value has come from soliciting and offering help, advice, and opinions. Through the Sportpsy list, you also may identify an individual with sufficient information or interest in a given topic for you to communicate extensively "off list" or through conventional e-mail communications.

World Wide Web

World Wide Web pages are a great source for obtaining information from professional organizations, universities, book publishers, sports organizations, and individuals. (See the Appendix for a list of some of these home pages relating to sport and sport psychology.) Once you know how to "surf the Net," you can search for and tap into resources from hundreds of Web pages related to almost any sport, psychological, or general interest topic. Web sites are usually interlinked, so when you tap into one resource, you automatically gain access to many others.

It is becoming increasingly easy and economical to have your own home page available to the world through the Internet. This can be a useful public information and marketing tool for your practice, as I discovered about a year ago when I created a home page for the Ohio Center for Sport Psychology (www.sportpsych.org).

QUALIFICATIONS AND CREDENTIALS

As you begin to expand your practice into new areas of sport psychology, ever mindful of the ethical and legal mandates that require you to practice within the limits of your competence, it is important that you be able to demonstrate your qualifications.

Qualifications

You must be able to answer the following question posed by potential clients, the public, and whatever licensing board governs your discipline: "How are you qualified to do what you're doing?" Unless you return to the university and obtain a degree in sport psychology, you are responsible for obtaining and documenting your qualifications.

If you've been carrying out self-directed educational activities such as those suggested in this chapter, keep a record of these activities. Especially in your early ventures, when your experience is limited, you might wish to keep a log of books read, consultations with other professionals, and attendance at conferences and workshops. Some workshops and seminars provide certificates of completion and continuing-education credits. Many of these activities will make important additions to your vita.

Less formally, but of no less significance, develop important qualifications by presenting your thinking and your work to those who are knowledgeable and are in a position to challenge or endorse what you're doing. There are two different types of groups here. The first are groups that you may already belong to, such as your local, state, or national professional organizations or sport psychological organizations. Second are groups within the athletic community.

For example, if you're working with figure skaters and believe that you've developed appropriate qualifications, give a presentation to a meeting of figure skating coaches. This is a good learning opportunity to validate what you've been doing and obtain useful feedback for further improvement.

In the end, qualification is an ongoing process, not an end result. For each activity, for each client, for each sport, and for each intervention, ask yourself, "To what extent am I qualified to do this?"

AAASP Certified Consultant

The only organization that has a certification program for sport psychologists is AAASP. After many years of debating the issue of who is qualified to function independently as a qualified sport psychologist, AAASP created the concept of Certified Consultant in 1991. The term deliberately avoids the word *psychology* or *psychologist* because many persons who are highly qualified have their degree in sport sciences, not psychology. They are therefore ineligible for licensure in psychology and are prohibited from identifying themselves as psychologists.

A certification program is an approach to the qualification question in which a set of standards is adopted by an organization (usually after considerable debate); then individuals who wish to be certified present evidence that they have met these standards. If a review board agrees with the evidence presented by the applicant, the individual is certified. Essentially the organization certifies that the individual has met the published standards. Unlike a license, a certificate does not permit a person to engage in any particular professional activities. However, potential employers of sport psychologists may require AAASP certification as a condition of employment. This has not yet happened on a large scale and may or may not happen in the future, for several reasons: the certification program is relatively new, the requirements still are not universally agreed on, not all well-qualified sport psychologists belong to AAASP, and many sport psychologists who would qualify for certification have not applied because they personally find no benefit to being certified at this time. Recently the U.S. Olympic Committee has strengthened the importance of AAASP Certified Consultant program by requiring applicants to its Sport Psychology Registry to have this certification, plus be an active member of the American Psychological Association.

The AAASP standards are high and add substantially to the credentials of those who are certified. Even if you're just beginning your involvement with sport psychology, become familiar with these standards because they specify what types of knowledge and experiences are deemed important to the practice of sport psychology. You may also use these standards to assess your own capabilities and set goals for your continued development.

In order to become a Certified Consultant (CC, AAASP), you must meet the following requirements:

Education

A doctoral degree from an accredited university

Coursework in Specific Areas

Knowledge of professional ethics and standards

Knowledge of sport psychology subdisciplines (intervention/ performance enhancement, health/exercise psychology, and social psychology)

Knowledge of the biomechanical and/or physiological bases of sport

Knowledge of the historical, philosophical, social, or motor behavioral bases of sports skills

Knowledge of psychopathology and its assessment

Knowledge and skills in research design, statistics, and psychological assessment

Of the following four criteria, each must be met through educational experiences that focus on general psychological principles (rather than sport-specific ones):

- Knowledge of the biological bases of behavior
- Knowledge of the cognitive-affective bases of behavior
- Knowledge of the social bases of behavior
- Knowledge of individual behavior

Supervised Practica and Other Supervised Experiences

Training designed to foster basic skills in counseling

Knowledge of skills and techniques within sport or exercise

Supervised experience, with a qualified person, during which the individual receives training in the use of sport psychology principles and techniques, at least 400 hours.

*Sustained Involvement Within the Profession,
as Evidenced by Some Combination of the Following:*

Professional contributions to applied sport psychology

Professional development experiences

Publications in sport psychology

Professional honors/memberships

References

Agreement to adhere to ethical standards

For additional information or to apply for certification, contact: Dr. Bonnie Berger, AAASP Certification Committee Chair, College of Health Sciences, Room 220, Ivinson Building, University of Wyoming, Laramie, Wyoming 82071–3432. Phone: (307) 766–2494; e-mail: bberger@uywo.edu.

Professional Ethics in Sport Psychology

As you begin to expand your practice into this new arena, review the ethics of your profession in general and specifically in regard to practicing within the limits of your competence. These principles may be useful in balancing your increasing competency with your increasing expansion into new activities with new clients.

In addition to the ethics of your own profession, AAASP has formulated a set of ethical guidelines for its membership. Although AAASP membership and adhering to these guidelines is voluntary, it is worthwhile for you to be familiar with them. These guidelines were ratified in October 1996 and will be available soon through the organization.

In an applied discipline such as sport psychology, professional development often follows a leapfrogging process. Learning leads to new application, then more learning, then more new application. Doing this in a gradual manner, with appropriate feedback from colleagues, is a relatively safe and effective means of expanding professional skills into new areas.

In the following chapters, I recommend tactics for implementing a gradual expansion of your practice into sport psychology. I start with services closest to the ones that you're already providing and suggest additional therapeutic interventions using movement and exercise and sport psychology principles in working with your current clinical clients. Later, I explore how to expand your clientele to athletes ranging from the casual recreational athlete to the elite.

3

Using Exercise in the
Treatment of Your Clinical Clients

*I can't believe I enjoy it. I look forward to it. I was
never an exerciser or athlete. I was always the last
one picked for a team in gym class. Now I'm doing
the treadmill every day and feel like I'm accomplishing
something. I'm actually feeling good, so it's not just
the results. I'm pleased with myself.*

Marie, age fifty-nine

Marie came to me three weeks ago, twenty-five pounds overweight, mildly depressed, and suffering from low self-esteem.
As part of our counseling process, which includes a behavior mod-
ification program to help her alter her eating habits, we discussed
the physical and mental benefits of regular exercise. Although she
and her husband had purchased a treadmill several years ago, neither had ever used it. Now, for the first time in her life, Marie was
discovering for herself that regular exercise is just as good for the
mind as it is for the body.

Although the main focus of this book is sport psychology, in this
chapter we will look at the contribution of exercise as an adjunct
to counseling with your current clinical clients. Exercise is a logical first step in a progression that can lead to recreational and serious sport participation. Exercise involves prescribed movement,
with anticipated benefits. Unlike sports, there are no rigid rules,

competitors, winners, and performance pressures. Although sport usually requires exercise, exercise does not require sport.

PHYSICAL AND PSYCHOLOGICAL BENEFITS OF EXERCISE

Studies have documented that regular, appropriate physical activity or exercise is important to one's overall health and fitness. Summarizing the research on this subject, the Surgeon General's recent report on physical activity and health (U.S. Department of Health and Human Services, 1996) included the following statements:

Regular physical activity that is performed on most days of the week reduces the risk of developing or dying from some of the leading causes of illness and death in the United States. Regular physical activity improves health in the following ways:

- Reduces the risk of dying prematurely.
- Reduces the risk of dying from heart disease.
- Reduces the risk of developing diabetes.
- Reduces the risk of developing high blood pressure.
- Helps reduce blood pressure in people who already have high blood pressure.
- Reduces the risk of developing colon cancer.
- Reduces feelings of depression and anxiety.
- Helps control weight.
- Helps build and maintain healthy bones, muscles, and joints.
- Helps older adults become stronger and better able to move about without falling.
- Promotes psychological well-being.

Given the numerous health benefits of physical activity, the hazards for being inactive are clear. Physical inactivity is a serious, nationwide problem. Its scope poses a public health challenge for reducing the national burden of unnecessary illness and premature death.

More recently, we have become aware of the equally impressive benefits of exercise to mental health. In the References listing, at the end of this chapter, you'll find several excellent summaries of the research on this topic. In spite of debate among researchers regarding methodology, correlation versus cause and effect, and other issues, the International Society of Sport Psychology (1992) issued a position statement on exercise and mental health that includes the following findings:[1]

- Exercise is associated with reduced state anxiety.
- Exercise has been associated with a decreased level of mild to moderate depression.
- Long-term exercise is usually associated with reductions in traits such as neuroticism and anxiety.
- Exercise may be an adjunct to the professional treatment of severe depression.
- Exercise results in the reduction of various stress indices.
- Exercise has beneficial emotional effects across all ages and in both sexes.

EXERCISE AS AN ADJUNCT TO PSYCHOTHERAPY

I began recommending exercise to my clinical clients shortly after discovering the psychological benefits of running in my own life. At that time I was developing three highly structured, individual programs to help clients quit smoking, lose weight, or manage stress more effectively. Based on my own experience, as well as the research literature, I incorporated exercise recommendations into each of these programs. Since that time, when appropriate, I have recommended exercise to clients who have come for more traditional psychotherapy, especially for those who are dealing with problems of anxiety, depression, and low self-esteem. Comprehensive reviews of research studies (Morgan, 1997; Leith, 1994) have supported the value of exercise for each of these three conditions.

Specific Requirements for Psychological Benefit

In addition to providing an excellent review of the literature, Larry Leith (1994) makes specific and separate recommendations for effective exercise intervention with depression, anxiety, and self-esteem. The recommendations for each of the three conditions are so similar that I have consolidated them into one list:

> *Type of exercise:* Running and walking appear to be quite effective; some studies have also found positive results with swimming, cycling, and weight lifting (especially for self-esteem)
>
> *Frequency:* Three to four times a week
>
> *Duration:* Fifteen to thirty minutes per session
>
> *Intensity:* Mild to moderate
>
> *Minimum time:* Ten to twelve weeks
>
> *Improvement in fitness:* Improvement in cardiovascular fitness does not seem to be prerequisite for psychological improvement to occur.
>
> *Aerobic versus anaerobic:* There appears to be no difference in psychological benefit.

Introducing Exercise to Clinical Clients

Most clients come to me already believing they should exercise. They have read countless articles in newspapers and magazines about the benefits of exercise, and many have been advised by their physicians to begin exercising. Nevertheless, most are not exercising at the time of their first visit with me. Many have made short-lived attempts at exercise sometime in the past, usually with inadequate information, preparation, commitment, and results. Many of these clients think of themselves as "nonexercisers" who cannot change.

Although the majority understand the physical benefits of exercise, only a few are aware of the psychological benefits. Clients who come to me for weight control are usually the least surprised at my exercise recommendation; those who come for help in dealing with depression and anxiety are usually the most surprised.

If you wish to add exercise as an adjunct to counseling, when appropriate, with your clinical clients, you might begin by examining your own exercise habits. The fact that you're interested in integrating sport psychology in your practice suggests that you're already likely to be participating in sports or exercise. Use your own experiences as a role model for your clients when this is appropriate. When I think it will be helpful, I share my own "transformation" story with my clients: how I took up running, quit smoking, lost weight, and changed psychologically. I also jokingly tell them that this is my form of "craziness" and that they don't need to run sixty miles a week or compete in marathons in order to benefit from exercise.

Here's a good example from my practice in which a client who began exercising experienced both predicted and unpredicted psychological benefits:

Lois was twenty-nine, had never been married, and was in the midst of a huge personal crisis when she made her first appointment with me. Her boyfriend of three years had just told her to move out. She presented a frail, almost sickly appearance, and she spoke in a whisper. She cried frequently during our first few sessions and was very depressed, although not suicidal. Lois had a long history of unsatisfactory relationships with men, starting with her father, who had physically abused her sister in her presence and was unusually harsh and critical of Lois during her growing-up years. No matter what she did, she was never able to please him. She had deeply internalized these feelings of inadequacy, and in spite of graduating from college and obtaining a professional job, she remained highly dependent on others, especially males, for her self-esteem.

Lois had had three long-lasting male relationships, each based on her becoming overly dependent emotionally on a strong male figure. Although all of these relationships were unhealthy, the sequence of them suggested some progress in her personal growth: the first boyfriend physically abused her, the second one verbally abused her, and the third did neither but lost interest in her and found another partner. Each of the three relationships had been terminated by the man, even though she was quite unhappy and well aware that she should have taken action to end it herself.

At the time of our first session, Lois was very upset about the recent breakup of her third relationship and anxious about living alone and not having a male partner. Shortly after finding an apartment, she became very depressed, especially on Friday and Saturday evenings when she was home alone. With an unsupportive family and few friends, she began drinking on these occasions and had an occasional sexual encounter with the apartment custodian, which would assuage her emotional pain at the moment but would result in considerable guilt the next morning. Depressed and feeling very unattractive, she was unable to reach out and develop new, healthy relationships.

After several months of therapy in which she began to understand some of her recurrent behavior patterns, especially with males, she still remained significantly depressed and continued her heavy drinking on weekend evenings. At this time, I suggested exercise to her as an adjunct to our therapy and provided her with information about the physical and psychological benefits that could be attained. Although open to the suggestion, she was not inclined toward some of the more usual aerobic exercises. Nevertheless, she began brisk walking a few days later and did it regularly in a dutiful, but not particularly pleasurable, way. She reported that this exercise did help her to feel a little better, but it was not enough.

Shortly after, she came to one of our weekly sessions more enthused than I had ever seen her before. She showed me an ad from the local newspaper seeking men and women who were interested in joining an after-work rowing club. For whatever reason, this had grabbed her attention. With only a small amount of encouragement from me, she followed through and went to the organizational meeting. Soon she was attending practices three times a week and preparing for competitions on the weekends.

A month later, Lois looked like a different person. Healthy color had returned to her once-pallid face, and she walked with a purpose. She talked enthusiastically about how it felt to be rowing hard, sweating, being out of breath, and finally experiencing the joyful relief that comes at the finishing line. At one point she stood up and proudly insisted that I feel her flexed biceps. We laughed together at how she was becoming a "jock." As an unanticipated, but important, fringe benefit, she was enjoying and earning the respect of new friends, both male and female, who valued health and exercise. This made it easier for her to give up alcohol and cigarette smoking. She began doing weight training at home, and on Friday and Saturday evenings, if she wasn't going out, she could now be comfortable at home, going to bed early so that she could be at practice or competition early the next morning.

Although there were still occasional recurrences of depression, these became both less frequent and less severe as time passed. In our therapy we used these recent positive experiences as anchors for a new way of building self-esteem, based on her own evaluation of herself rather than that of others. The rowing enabled Lois to feel more grounded in herself and in her abilities. We related this to other life goals and developing assertive strategies for accomplishing them. Most important, Lois was no longer afraid of living alone, which enabled her to become more selective with male companions and, we both hoped, avoid abusive relationships.

When Exercise Is Appropriate

The most appropriate clients for using exercise as an adjunct to therapy are those whose goals are to quit smoking, lose weight, or manage stress more effectively or those with depression, anxiety, or self-esteem problems. Both the research and my clinical experience have demonstrated the value of exercise in attaining these goals.

As part of my initial assessment of all new clients, I obtain information about their current and past health problems, surgeries, and medications. If there is any indication of possible medical risk related to exercise, such as undiagnosed chest pains or joint pains, I refer the individual to his or her personal physician before beginning any exercise program. This is a rare occurrence. In fact, it is more likely that a physician has referred the client to me for help in developing healthier life habits that include exercise.

Because of the particular nature of my practice and the clients who are referred, I probably recommend exercise to approximately half of all my clients. About half of these will accept this recommendation and initiate a serious exercise program. About half of these will succeed in maintaining exercise as a permanent part of their life.

Tom is a good example of a client who dropped out of exercise because of his impulsivity and poor time management skills. As a highly intense Type A personality, he stopped at a local sporting goods store on the way home immediately after our second session to purchase a pair of the most expensive running shoes and several complete running outfits. The following morning he ran two miles before going to work and did so each day for two weeks. Just as quickly as he started, his brief exercise career came to an abrupt halt. In order to run in the morning, he was arriving late at his job and had developed a backlog of work. Although he promised himself to return to running as soon as he caught up on his work, this never occurred during the six months that he remained in therapy.

On the other hand, Sue, a twenty-six-year-old single mother of a preschooler, joined a health club near her place of work. She successfully negotiated with her supervisor to start work a half-hour late and reduce her lunch break accordingly in order to "work out" each morning. Although exercise was uncomfortable and painful for her during the first three weeks, she maintained the commitment she'd made to herself. After about a month, she found herself looking forward to her morning exercise routine and was upset on the few occasions that she had to miss it.

Bolstering Client Motivation

The first step in introducing exercise to nonexercising clients is to assess their current motivation and find ways to bolster it. Those with a recent history of positive exercise experiences are usually the most receptive to the recommendation of exercise as part of their therapy. Other clients have already been advised by their physicians to exercise for reasons of physical health and for preventing or treating medical problems such as obesity and hypertension. They may feel guilty for not exercising but don't know what to do or how to get started. You can channel this guilt in a positive direction by providing the structure and information that they need in order to be successful.

As a therapist, you will want to link exercise with the client's psychological goals. Your client may be totally unaware of the demonstrated benefits of exercise for problems of depression, anxiety, and self-esteem, so providing this information is essential. This may be as simple as a brief explanation of the research findings, or you may wish to develop a handout for this purpose or photocopy short articles from reputable newspapers and magazines.

Many of my clients have specifically chosen to come to a non-medical therapist for treatment of anxiety or depression because they wish to avoid treatment that includes the use of psychotropic medications. Some have had negative experiences with medication, or have unusual sensitivities, or are fearful of the side effects. Others don't believe that medication is an effective long-range solution to their life problems. These clients are especially motivated toward exercise as an adjunct to psychotherapy.

Overcoming Client Resistance

Regardless of motivational level, most clients come with some resistance to exercise that you will need to address. "I just don't have the time" is a quite common explanation. Those with a recent exercise "failure" experience present the greatest resistance. In these instances, I ask for a detailed description of their experience. Usually the story that I hear is one of a highly impulsive decision, no clear plan, considerable discomfort, and no results. Often exercise was part of a crash program to lose weight, precipitated by an approaching daughter's wedding, a television ad for exercise equipment, or the unbridled enthusiasm of a friend. Others, such as Maria, quoted at the beginning of this chapter, have a self-concept in which they just don't see themselves as athletic or as the "type" of person who exercises.

After assessing the client's resistance to exercise, the issues the person raises need to be addressed in a positive manner. I make it clear that, although strongly recommended, exercise is not a mandatory part of our therapy. If the client is willing to try exercise, I will ask him or her to commit to a trial of four weeks before evaluating it. My experience has shown that most clients who can be persuaded to exercise regularly for four weeks will have experienced sufficient positive feelings to continue with little outside pressure.

Establishing Realistic Goals

The exercise goal that I recommend for optimum physical and mental health benefits is to engage in an aerobic exercise for at least thirty minutes a day, every day. I emphasize that this is the *goal*, not the starting point, and that there are many pathways leading to that goal. First, encourage the client to choose the type of aerobic exercise that has some appeal—for example, walking, jogging, treadmill, stair machine, exercycle, swimming, or aerobic classes, records, or videotapes. If the client has no preference whatsoever, I generally recommend brisk walking, which appears to be the most convenient, safest, and easiest exercise for most people. Or a client may wish to alternate among several modes of aerobic exercise on different days.

The client begins with low levels of duration, frequency, and intensity and gradually increases each, in that order, to reduce the risk of overdoing it and experiencing soreness, injury, or displeasure. Maintaining the exercise habit is almost as difficult as getting it started, so early negative experiences can be very discouraging and can weaken the client's commitment. I much prefer a client's "underdoing" it at first, but enjoying and persisting in the new activity. Initially I recommend starting the exercise at a low level of intensity and stopping at the earliest signs of discomfort. Whatever that duration is (even three minutes), the client needs to repeat it every other day for a week. The following week, if he or she feels all right, add two minutes to the duration of the session and make that the new goal for each session during that week. Each week, repeat that procedure until the full thirty minutes is reached. Depending on their age, level of fitness, and health, some of my clients choose to exercise initially every day; others prefer to exercise every other day until they feel more fit.

As a long-term advocate of shaping, the reinforcement of successive approximations, I am comfortable with any improvement over the client's current (nonexistent) level of exercise, at least as a starting point. If a client wishes to exercise three minutes every Monday and that's all, that would be fine with me as a start. But that doesn't seem to happen; most clients want to make a commitment, exert an effort, and experience results in a relatively short period of time. This is exactly what happened with Jonathan.

Jonathan had been an unusually gifted, precocious, and lonely child. Now, at age forty, he was experiencing a high level of professional success. A prominent attorney, he had published several books in his specialty, developed a national reputation, and was in great demand on the lecture circuit. Nevertheless, he had haunting doubts about his abilities.

At the same time that his career was blossoming, his personal life was in shambles. For twelve years, Jonathan had been married, with no children, to a highly creative, temperamental artist whose pottery was featured in prominent magazines and displayed in major galleries. From the beginning, she had dominated the relationship through her strong will and frequent emotional outbursts. He was quiet and reserved; she was flamboyant and outgoing. Because of his introversion and aloof manner, he had few friends, and she had become his main source of social contact. During the past few years, she had become vicious in her continued criticism of his appearance, his work, and his sexual prowess. These tirades, which made him furious at her, reinforced the self-doubts that had plagued him for most of his life.

Jonathan came to therapy to find the support and courage to end his marriage, as well as to overcome his self-doubts. The couple had attempted marital therapy a few years before, and Jonathan was quite adamant that he wanted to end the marriage, not save it. As part of my intake, I administered a battery of psychological tests, the results of which were essentially within normal limits. When I shared these results with him, Jonathan was quite astonished that I did not corroborate his wife's opinion that he was seriously emotionally disturbed. Many times during the year that I worked with him, he referred back to the favorable test results and how they had begun to change his self-perceptions. About a month after therapy began, he found the courage to ask his wife for a divorce. She agreed with little hesitation, but threatened to make large financial demands.

After moving into his own apartment, Jonathan started to become quite anxious, anticipating the absolute worst. With time on his hands now, he began to worry more and more about his future and could only see disastrous scenarios. He was losing sleep and having significant difficulty concentrating on the job. His personal physician had recommended sleeping pills, but Jonathan was opposed. He had been a vegetarian most of his adult life and wanted to find a "more natural" way of reducing his anxiety and sleeping better. It was at this time that I suggested the therapeutic use of exercise.

Jonathan was open to the suggestion and sought additional information from me as well as other sources. After a week, he purchased a bicycle, helmet, and riding clothing and soon developed a daily plan. He had no resistance to exercise and proceeded in a methodical manner, characteristic of how he approached most matters in his life. Each week he enjoyed sharing his exercise log with me and was pleased to report he had experienced a highly welcomed weight loss as well. The first benefit that he noticed was a substantial improvement in his ability to fall asleep and remain asleep. Once well rested, he was able to improve his work concentration and feel better about himself and his productivity. As he began to develop confidence in the strength and integrity of his body, he began to feel more confident in his overall capacity to deal with life challenges.

This turned out to be a long-term therapy case with a positive ending. Over the next few years, Jonathan and his wife were divorced, he began dating, he made some risky but successful career changes, and ultimately he remarried. At last contact, he was doing well, personally and professionally, and was still riding his bicycle at least four times a week.

Commitment to the Daily Plan

After making my recommendations, the client and I discuss her preferences for an exercise program that will be enjoyable, realistic, and beneficial. My goal is for her to use the information that I've provided to create and commit to a program that she will experience as her own. Some people are comfortable exercising at home on their own, either with or without equipment, while others prefer the organized classes and companionship that health clubs provide.

Once the major decisions are made—type of exercise, duration, frequency, and intensity—it's time to help the client design a daily plan, the core of a successful exercise program. This is the most important missing ingredient in many failed exercise attempts. The daily plan translates the overall program into very specific commitments with regard to behavior, time, and place. These are the dimensions of all behaviors and the key to successful habit change in any arena.

Often clients seriously neglect to define the specific, daily behaviors necessary to attain the goal even when they are highly committed to their goal. For example, if John's plan says, "I'll exercise on the weekend," it probably won't happen. If he states, "I'll jog on Saturday," the odds improve. However, if he commits, "I'll jog thirty minutes on Saturday morning, beginning at 7:30, in my neighborhood," he is most likely to carry out his commitment. This is effective for many reason, one of which is directly derived from effective sport psychology techniques: "If you want to do it, imagine yourself doing it." Try this exercise on yourself right now. What kind of image comes to your mind with the words, "I'll exercise on the weekend"? Vague images, at best, I would suppose. Notice how the specificity of your imagery improves when you say, "I'll jog thirty minutes on Saturday morning, beginning at 7:30, in my neighborhood."

I encourage clients to formulate a plan for a week at a time, understanding that they may make changes, preferably in advance, as they go. Some prefer to plan one day ahead, which is also all right. One way of presenting the importance of a plan to clients who believe that they have difficulty in making and carrying out such commitments is to demonstrate that they are already doing so successfully in another area of their lives. I may say to a client, for example, something like, "This is the tenth time you've had an appointment with me. You made each appointment in advance. You have kept all of your appointments, and you have always been on time. Once, when you were sick, you called me early that morning and rescheduled for later in the week. You have been very conscientious in making and keeping appointments with me. I bet you could be just as effective in making and keeping appointments with yourself." Rarely has this explanation failed to obtain a positive response.

The daily plan, then, is a series of appointments that the client makes with himself in order to carry out exercise that is specified in advance with respect to behavior, time, and place. In order to be successful, the client must make a strong commitment to the plan rather than to the overall, long-range goals. Commitment to overall goals may make clients feel good but has little effect on the behaviors necessary to accomplish them. An analogy from work with athletes is apropos here: "Focus on your behavior; winning will take care of itself."

Maintaining the Exercise Behavior

Once the client begins exercising by following the daily plan, the next consideration is maintaining the behavior, especially during the early days when the physical discomforts may be abundant and reinforcement minimal. The less physically fit the individual is, the longer it will take before exercise begins to "feel good" and become self-reinforcing. In the interim, self-monitoring and reinforcement during therapy sessions will be important in maintaining the new and somewhat fragile behaviors. I furnish most clients with a self-monitoring log sheet in which they record their compliance with their daily plan along with subjective comments. It's often helpful to have the client generate a summary statistic that will provide a feeling of accomplishment. Depending on the type of exercise, it might be something like, "I exercised a total of twelve hours during the month of March" or "I walked two hundred miles, the distance from New York City to Boston, between March and June."

Fortunately, in many cases, the psychological benefits are often evident very soon after the client begins to exercise. The physical exertion, which may feel good and be reinforcing in itself, often is accompanied by important cognitive changes, such as, "Now I'm actually doing something that I've wanted to do for a long time." Clients begin to get the positive feelings associated with the setting of a goal, devising a plan, and carrying out that plan. This is good medicine for self-esteem and a wonderful antidote for the feelings of helplessness, depression, anxiety, and low self-esteem that these clients bring to us. Later, the same process may be generalized to the client's other goals.

Integrating Exercise and Psychotherapy

Kate Hays (1993), in an excellent review of the use of exercise in psychotherapy, defines three possible roles for the therapist: consultant, role model, and participant. The consultant role is the one developed and described in detail in this chapter. In the second mode, the role model, the therapist shares information about his or her own exercise experiences with the client. I have found this to be effective, if used judiciously. While I am comfortable sharing some of the highlights of my own exercise experiences with my clients, I emphasize the early days, my transition from a sedentary person to a beginning runner, the hopeful aspect of my experience with which I would like my client to identify. I deliberately downplay my marathon experiences, which may evoke feelings of intimidation or competition, neither of which is productive. Finally, there are a few instances reported in which the therapist is a fellow participant in the exercise, such as jogging with a client or group of clients.

Hays discusses advantages, disadvantages, and issues associated with each of these roles. As one progresses from consultant to role model and especially to participant, the customary client-therapist relationship is altered. For example, in running with a client as part of therapy, the therapeutic relationship becomes free of the usual constraints of both office and tradition. Although this provides an opportunity for a more natural, authentic relationship with the client, it also raises the concerns about interpersonal boundaries, competition between client and therapist, therapist's personal disclosure, dual relationships, confidentiality, and legal liabilities. Nevertheless, I believe these issues should challenge, rather than deter, the mature, seasoned therapist to use this modality as an aspect of psychotherapy. Unfortunately, such creativity today seems to go against the grain of standardized therapy protocols endorsed by insurance and managed care companies.

In order to ensure that the exercise is producing the intended therapeutic effect, it is necessary to spend some of the therapeutic time discussing the client's experiences. When I am able, I get clients to keep a journal that includes recording their thoughts and feelings before, during, and after exercise, as well as those related to these clients' other therapy goals. These logs become topics of discussion during therapy sessions, and I am especially interested in clients' spontaneous references to psychological changes associated with the exercise, especially changes in depression, anxiety, and self-esteem. I also look for generalizations from the exercise to other life experiences. For example, a woman I worked with several years ago became a regular and serious walker. She reported feeling first physically stronger, then mentally stronger, and then began acting more assertively with her supervisor and fellow employees.

As in my own running experience, many clients are pleasantly surprised at an alteration of consciousness that they sometimes experience while exercising. This seems to be especially likely in such rhythmic activities as brisk walking and running, where the stream of consciousness may be similar to free association and lead to insights and creative thoughts relevant to the therapy. I encourage the client to record such thoughts in a journal so that they may be remembered and discussed later in our counseling sessions.

Psychological Risks of Exercise

As with any other treatment modality, exercise is not without its risks. In addition to the obvious physical risks, such as injury or exacerbating an existing medical condition, there are psychological risks as well. The therapist who recommends exercise as an adjunct to therapy needs to do so within the context of a nonjudgmental therapeutic milieu so that therapy itself is not jeopardized if the client rejects the exercise recommendation. Similarly, the client needs to feel free to quit or fail at the exercise experience without worrying about the therapist's disapproval or compromising therapy. Indeed, exercise must be viewed as an adjunct to therapy. Therapy itself is the prime intervention and must not be compromised.

Another possible risk is that the exercise itself is carried to an excess and comes to assume a psychologically unhealthy place in the client's life. During the running boom of the 1980s, there were reports of individuals who had become "addicted" to running and seriously neglected other important areas of their lives, such as family, work, and even their own health. Exercise itself can, under some circumstances, become an escape from life problems rather than an effective coping mechanism. This is illustrated in the case of Pete.

Pete was overwhelmed with stress when he began therapy. At age thirty-two, he had been married for seven years and had two young children. His wife, ambitious and hard working, had quickly reached a high administrative level in her organization. Pete, less intense and more casual, worked as a technician. Although he liked his job and was competent, he felt intimidated by his wife's success. Since she worked longer hours and was an administrator by nature, she demanded that he play a major role in child care and home management. He dealt with these roles in a passive-aggressive manner and seldom asserted himself in her presence. Occasionally he would have an angry outburst, to which she would retaliate with critical verbiage that he couldn't match.

Pete had been a lifelong sports fan and had previously played baseball and basketball. Now, with family and job responsibilities, he was unable to find the time to play in a league, but he thought some type of involvement with sports would be of benefit to him. After some discussion, he decided to start running to reduce his anxiety and increase his self-esteem. I provided him with encouragement as well as handouts on how to start running safely. He quickly became dedicated to his daily plan, and then began to increase his duration, frequency, and intensity at an unhealthy rate. I shared my concern with him, but it was not heeded. Soon, before he was adequately trained, Pete was beginning to compete in five-mile and ten-kilometer races. He was driven and pushed himself into severe discomfort. It took considerable effort on my part to direct our therapy content away from the details of his training programs and running shoes. Pete's interest and commitment to therapy waned, and his attendance became erratic.

Pete received little external reinforcement for his running. In spite of his efforts, he didn't train or race properly and never ran impressive times, even within his age group. His wife, who at first gave strong support to this activity, began to object when he neglected his household and child care duties in order to train and race. Although Pete felt somewhat self-righteous about his commitment to his sport, he stubbornly refused to accept the advice of other runners or myself. After about six months, to no one's great surprise, he developed foot problems that eventually caused him to stop running altogether. He became resentful and angry and discontinued his therapy prematurely.

Exercise and Relationship Changes

The psychological benefits of exercise may extend beyond improvements in depression, anxiety, and self-esteem into the realm of relationships as well. A good example of this is the case of Vicky, in which exercise and psychotherapy helped her discover and change her unhealthy dependency on her husband.

At age forty-five Vicky seemed to have lost purpose in life. She had married her childhood sweetheart immediately after high school and soon became pregnant with the first of their two children. Bob was hard working and achieved early success with his company, a large, national corporation. With his substantial income, it was unnecessary for Vicky to seek employment. She was a good homemaker and took great pride in raising their children. Her mother, whom she described as her "best friend," lived nearby and was a daily part of her life.

Six months before starting therapy with me, Vicky's life has taken a sudden, unexpected turn for the worse. Her husband's company had met with severe financial difficulties and was in the process of downsizing. Bob was given the choice between terminating his employment or accepting a relocation with a substantial pay cut. Agreeing to the latter, the family soon found itself with less money and in a new, strange city, a thousand miles away from their long-time home.

While Bob's energies became focused on succeeding at his new job assignment, the job also provided him with instant social contacts as well as new golf partners. He spent long hours at the job and played more golf than usual as a means of socializing and reducing his stress. Vicky, however, had lost the beautiful home that she had created over the years, along with the closeness of her mother and other lifelong friends. Her younger child, a daughter, had left for college, and her son, a high school junior, was striving for his independence. She now found herself in a modest home with no decorating budget and much time on her hands. She regretted not having developed skills that would have enabled her to find employment. Feeling unneeded by her husband and children, distanced from her mother and friends, and incapable of decorating her house or finding work, she became withdrawn and depressed, and these emotional difficulties prevented her from going out and making new friends.

In our therapy, it soon became apparent that Vicky fit many of the descriptions of the Avoidant Personality Disorder. Her earlier lifestyle had camouflaged many of her unresolved conflicts that were now coming to the light in a painful way. Before we could address these lifelong issues, however, it was necessary to deal with the debilitating feelings of depression that were preventing her from becoming more active and assertive. After seeing only a minimal response to a cognitive-behavioral approach, I recommended either a medication consultation with a psychiatrist or an exercise program. Having played tennis many years before, Vicky was open to accepting physical exercise as a means of reducing the depression. As with Marie, quoted at the opening of this chapter, she and Bob had purchased but never used a treadmill.

The following week, Vicky began walking on the treadmill every other day for about seven minutes, her limit of comfort at the time. She reported immediate positive feelings and was very proud of herself for initiating a new and strenuous activity. She logged each of her exercise sessions and within a month had gradually increased her time to fifteen minutes and was beginning to exercise daily. The treadmill commitment enabled her to get up early each morning, exercise, shower, dress, and start her day. She soon found creative and economical ways of redecorating her house and began slowly to make new friends.

In therapy, Vicky came to realize how domineering Bob had been to her, and she started standing up for herself and her needs more often than in the past. For a long time, Bob had talked about exercising on the treadmill but never got around to it. In this one area of her life, Vicky had done something that he had not been able to do. This felt good to her, and it appeared that he came to respect her for this, something he had never imagined possible.

A year after she began, Vicky was still exercising on the treadmill every day. She was now walking briskly for an hour each time and once or twice a month had proudly walked ten miles without stopping. Considerably less depressed, she was now thinking about going back to school or doing volunteer work for an agency.

————

Both research and clinical experience demonstrate the use and benefits of exercise as an adjunct to psychotherapy, especially in dealing with issues of depression, anxiety, and self-esteem. This chapter has presented practical guidelines for introducing exercise as a treatment modality with your current clients, a good first step in integrating sport psychology in your practice. The next step in the progression is to look at how principles commonly used with athletes in attaining their goals may be useful in your work with clinical clients.

Note

1. Reprinted by permission from International Society of Sport Psychology, 1992, "Physical activity and psychological benefits," *The Sport Psychologist*, 6(2), p. 201.

References

Hays, K. F. (1993). The use of exercise in psychotherapy. In L. VanderCreek, S. Knapp, & T. L. Jackson (Eds.), *Innovations in clinical practice: A source book* (Vol. 12) (pp. 155–168). Sarasota, FL: Professional Resource Press.

International Society of Sport Psychology. (1992). Physical activity and psychological benefits: A position statement. *The Sport Psychologist*, 6(2), 199–203.

Leith, L. M. (1994). *Foundations of exercise and mental health*. Morgantown, WV: Fitness Information Technology.

Morgan, W. P. (Ed.). (1997). *Physical activity and mental health*. Washington, DC: Taylor & Francis.

U.S. Department of Health and Human Services. (1996). *Physical activity and health: A report of the surgeon general* (Order number 7895). Superintendent of Documents, P.O. Box 371954, Pittsburgh, PA 15250–7954.

4

Using Sport Psychology Techniques with Your Clinical Clients

At age sixty-six, Betty had been terrified of flying for most of her life and until recently had limited air travel to one or two times a decade. Now, she and her husband were retired, and their only child had moved from Ohio to California and recently given birth to their first grandchild. Eager to meet her new granddaughter, Betty was highly motivated to overcome her fear in order to make the lengthy trip by air.

At the time of her first visit with me, Betty proudly announced that she and her husband had already booked airline tickets to San Francisco, approximately six weeks from that date. She had been referred to me with high expectations by a friend, a former client of mine, specifically for help in reducing her anxieties for the upcoming trip and for overcoming this longstanding and restrictive fear. Her ticket purchase signaled great confidence in a favorable and timely outcome of the therapy that we were about to begin.

At the conclusion of our first session, after obtaining considerable information about her fear as well as other assessment data, I explained to Betty that I would work with her using some of the same techniques that I'd used successfully with athletes. The experiences that she had shared with me were comparable to what a high school gymnast might feel before competing in state finals or a professional football player a few days before a major playoff game. The commonality was fear, based not on immediate reality but on imagining the worst and then reacting to the images as if they were reality. When athletes learn to control their imagination, I explained to her, their anxieties are reduced. Betty responded positively to my reframing psychotherapy in this manner. She had come into my office thinking of herself as a "neurotic," as others had unkindly labeled her over the years, and she had left feeling like a "jock" who now had a "coach" to teach her skills for managing anxiety effectively.

INTRODUCING SPORT PSYCHOLOGY

In the previous chapter, I reviewed the use of physical exercise as an adjunct to psychotherapy and the resulting psychological benefits: improvements in depression, anxiety, and self-esteem. These benefits tend to be general, internal changes that the client carries to a wide variety of life situations. In contrast to this, the techniques discussed in this chapter go beyond exercise and can be viewed as preparing the client for effective "performance behavior in a demanding situation."

The Origin of Sport Psychology Techniques

Ultimately there are no unique "sport psychology techniques." This is a label of convenience, referring to a collection of practical performance-enhancement strategies that sport psychologists commonly teach in their work with athletes. They are derived from general principles of psychology and from specific applications of behaviorism and cognitive-behavioral and social learning theory. You may recognize some of the techniques that have been adapted from the clinical contributions of Albert Bandura, Aaron Beck, Joseph Cautela, Albert Ellis, Milton Erickson, Arnold Lazarus, Donald Meichenbaum, Julian Rotter, Joseph Wolpe, and many others. Most likely you are already using some of these techniques in your practice; others may be new to you, depending on your particular background and training.

The performance-enhancement techniques I describe are essentially client skills for effectively managing specific life situations.

The therapist's task is to teach these skills to the client and help the client use them effectively in life.

When Sport Psychology Is Appropriate

The application of these techniques to clinical clients is most useful when the client's therapy goals can be successfully defined in terms of a desired performance behavior in a demanding situation—for example, performing well on a job interview, acting assertively when being taken advantage of by others, or going into surgery relaxed and optimistic. Additionally, these techniques can be used in marital counseling where each partner can benefit from learning behaviors for deescalating conflict, focusing on specific issues, and managing anger in a healthy way. In the treatment of substance abuse, these sport psychology techniques can help the client reduce anxieties and deal more effectively with life's stressful situations without the use of chemicals.

These techniques are not particularly useful or appropriate for clients whose primary therapeutic goals are oriented toward such internal, abstract issues as value clarification, decision making, reduction of internal conflict, and existential issues, such as searching for meaning and purpose in life. Nor would these techniques be useful for seriously psychotic individuals with hallucinations and delusions.

Sport as Metaphor for Life

When I began expanding the sport psychology aspect of my practice, I became concerned that my identity with sports and athletes might compromise my clinical practice. I worried that as my clinical clients became aware of this specialization, they might question my skills, interest, and effectiveness in helping them with their clinical problems. Much to my surprise, the opposite has occurred. Like Betty, most of my clinical clients are comfortable with the mild sports decor of my office, the knowledge that I work intensively with athletes, and the occasional media attention that I receive for my sport psychology activities.

My clinical clients easily understand sports as a metaphor for life without the need for extensive explanation or discussion. They seem to understand intuitively and identify with the struggles and the challenges of athletes and teams from Little League to the professional ranks. Most are aware of the ever-changing dynamics of an athlete's goals, limited resources, obstacles, rules, penalties, successes, and failures. They especially respect the athletes and teams that strive diligently to perform their best even against great odds. As with Betty, it generally takes only a few words to establish a positive connection between the athlete's challenges and their own. Clearly clients do not have to be sports fans in order to appreciate this analogy.

This metaphor in many instances becomes the framework for the nonathlete's experiences with sport psychology. Unlike the medical or illness model, where the removal of symptoms is usually the goal, the sports framework is growth oriented, exciting, and positive. I seek to help clients go beyond symptom removal by helping them master specific life situations with a high level of competence. Clients come to understand that they will attain their goals through hard work, practice, and training, as athletes do. They accept the analogy that I can serve them as a type of coach who will provide analysis, training, and strategies, although in the end, they go out onto the playing field of life alone while I remain on the sidelines, unable to provide direct assistance.

Although the sport metaphor is useful and acceptable for many clients, I do not suggest it for everyone. Some people have a negative attitude toward sports and athletes or are totally uninformed about and disinterested in this area of life. Others may have had unpleasant experiences associated with sports that would make this framework uncomfortable and unacceptable for them. Like any other treatment approach, I offer the metaphor only when I think the client would be receptive to it and would benefit from viewing psychotherapy in this manner.

APPLYING PERFORMANCE-ENHANCEMENT TECHNIQUES WITH CLINICAL CLIENTS

With only four seconds left in the game and his team down by two points, a basketball player sinks a perfect three-point shot and his team wins the game.

A baseball player comes to bat with the bases loaded and two outs. After reaching a full count, he swings assuredly with all of his power and hits a grand-slam home run deep into the left field grandstand.

These are the great moments in sports that excite us and leave us with feelings of awe and inspiration. Performances such as these, under any conditions, require extraordinary anatomical gifts, extensive conditioning, and unusual athletic abilities. Under extreme pressure, they require an additional component: highly developed mental skills, the same mental skills associated with high levels of performance and success in other areas of life as well. We see examples in the performances of successful dancers, musicians, surgeons, airplane pilots, college students, and corporate executives. From sport psychology research, we know that these skills are identifiable, they can be learned, and they can be improved through training and practice. We know how to teach these skills and how to help athletes apply them in specific sports situations.

These are the same skills that are often underdeveloped in clinical clients who experience unusual difficulties in dealing with (or avoiding) specific life situations. In the remainder of this chapter, each of the major performance-enhancement techniques is introduced as it is typically employed by successful, elite athletes. Then we look at ways in which skill deficiencies in this area may result in adjustment problems for your clients and specific ways in which the techniques can be used as part of your psychotherapy.

Motivation

> Successful, elite athletes are aware of the benefits that they expect to
> experience through sport participation. They have the ability to persist
> through difficult tasks and difficult times, even when these benefits are
> not immediately forthcoming.

Unlike successful athletes, clients often come to us without a clear
understanding of their own motivation. And without this understanding, it's difficult for them to set goals, develop plans, focus their
actions, and experience the successful results of their efforts. The
only immediate motivation that they may experience is psychological discomfort, in the form of anxiety, depression, low self-esteem,
or confusion, which brought them into psychotherapy and for
which they desire immediate relief.

The psychological discomfort that may motivate the client
toward therapy is a primitive and undifferentiated motive that often
results from the client's failure to assess and act effectively in satisfying other more complex motivations. For example, psychological
discomfort may be the result of not having successfully identified
and fulfilled basic motivations for having friends, self-respect, inti-
macy, rewarding work, being comfortable with oneself, respect from
others, education, meaningful leisure activities, and so forth. Therefore, early in the therapy, the therapist and client address the primary question, "Beyond symptom removal, what does the client
really want [or need]?" The second question is, "How hard is the
client willing to work to get what she wants?" Client and therapist
approach these issues from many different points of view, using different techniques, depending on the therapist's theoretical preferences, training, and experiences. Without an understanding of the
client's motivation, it will be difficult to set meaningful, appropriate goals.

For Betty, the new grandmother who came to therapy in order
to overcome her fear of flying, her motivation was both clear and
powerful: she wanted to meet her new granddaughter. Had her

motivation been to overcome her fear of flying in order to accompany her husband on his annual visit to his elderly, cranky mother in a nursing home, Betty's motivational picture might have been quite different.

In other cases, motivation is not so clear. Translating the client's presenting problems into therapeutic goals without first examining underlying motivation can lead to inappropriate goal setting.

Bill and Tom, both high school juniors with high B grade-point averages, sought counseling in order to overcome severe test anxiety that each believes has seriously lowered his test scores. Both aspire to the high goal of getting all A's. After questioning, we discover that Bill's underlying motivation is to win the approval of his parents.

Now that his motivation has been identified, it becomes important to understand why Bill feels it necessary to win their approval. Has he felt that he has never had his parents' approval? Has he lost it? Does he have it and not know he has it? Would he in fact achieve it if he obtained all A's? Are there other, more effective ways of achieving parental approval? After a discussion with Bill, we might agree to focus our work on Bill's limited communication skills that have made it difficult for him to discuss and clarify these concerns with his parents. If this is favorably resolved, we may discover that with assurance of approval from his parents, the pressure to obtain all A's is gone and, with it, his test anxiety.

In contrast, Tom's motivation for all A's, we discover, derives from his desire to attain a full scholarship to a prestigious university. Thus, the connection between his immediate goal of reducing test anxiety and his underlying motivation of financial support for a quality education is clear, direct, and appropriate. In view of this, we designed a treatment program that taught Tom the skills for reducing his test anxiety and performing closer to his full potential on tests.

Setting and Achieving Goals

Successful, elite athletes are able to set long-term and short-term goals that are realistic, behavioral, measurable, and time oriented. They are able to assess their performance level and develop a specific, detailed plan for attaining their goals. They are able to identify and obtain the resources necessary to achieve the goal.

In many cases, clients benefit by learning how to become more effective in setting goals for themselves and how to develop and follow specific plans for attaining these goals. Many clients come to us with goals that are as well intended but as vague as last year's New Year's resolutions with respect to specificity and method. It's not unusual for me to hear clients express their determination to "become healthier," "get along better with my son," or "find a better job." Often they have entertained these desires for a long period of time, but the desires have not produced any specific, focused, and effortful action or appreciable results. If I inquire how they intend to accomplish these goals, the response is often, "I'll try harder." As we discussed in the previous chapter with regard to formulating good exercise habits, behavioral change is most likely to occur when the person is committed to a plan that requires a specific behavior, at a specific time, in a specific place. Without that, little change is likely.

The therapy itself is an excellent tool for teaching the client the skills of setting goals, developing a plan, and carrying out the plan. Near the conclusion of a first therapy session, I generally ask the client, "If we are successful, how will things be different for you when this therapy is completed?" Based on the client's response, we formulate specific, written goals. The next question, "How will we know whether you have reached these goals?" prompts a focus on behavioral specificity and a behavioral definition of outcome. Finally, querying, "What has to happen in order for you to reach these goals?" usually leads to the formulation of a plan in which I agree to provide suggestions, guidance, and feedback, and the client commits to engaging in specific actions according to a plan that the two of us will devise and revise in subsequent sessions. Before continuing, we set target dates for achieving the goal and for steps along the way.

Using this model and techniques of performance enhancement, the client usually expresses goals as "performance behaviors in performance situations." The client who comes with the vague goal of "becoming healthier," for example, now commits herself to several specific behaviors, such as "eating more fiber and less fat at mealtime" and "brisk walking for a half-hour each morning before leaving for work." "Getting along better with my son" becomes, "spending more time with my son on weekends" and "talking less and listening more to my son and reacting in a less judgmental manner."

Let's look at a typical case.

Helen was thirty-one years old, married, and with two children, one infant and one toddler. She was highly intelligent, unusually shy, spoke in a soft voice, and made only limited eye contact. Married to a very immature man, whom she described as her "third child," she knew that the marriage would end in divorce once the children were older and after she completed her college degree and was economically self-sufficient. She envisaged approximately five more years with Harold before this would come about. In the meantime, she wanted to cope more effectively with what she called his "tantrum behavior."

Whenever he became frustrated, such as cutting himself while shaving, Harold would run to her and yell and scream profanities. Although he never physically abused her, and she believed that he was highly unlikely to, his verbal behavior was very frightening and upsetting to her. Whenever he was at home, she anticipated that he could "go off" without warning, and she consequently remained in a high state of anxiety and had difficulty eating, sleeping, relaxing, and enjoying her children.

Helen's initial goal was simply "to feel more comfortable at home." After some discussion, this was refined to "feel more comfortable at home when Harold is home," since she was, in fact, quite comfortable at home as long as he wasn't there. After a few sessions, I suggested to Helen that we focus on a "performance behavior in a performance situation." Harold's tantrum behavior would define the performance situation, to which her corresponding performance behavior would be an "effective, assertive response."

For Helen this indeed was a high-pressure situation that demanded a high-level performance. From her perspective, she was not unlike the basketball player who has the ball, with his team two points behind and four seconds remaining in the game. In fact, I would argue that the pressure on her was even greater because this was real life, with serious and enduring consequences to her and her children. We both believed that if she could develop an effective behavior for this situation, she would no longer live in fear of Harold's outbursts. Two important considerations influenced the performance behavior that we ultimately decided on: her strong belief that he was unlikely to harm her physically and his unblemished work record, with no history of outbursts on the job.

The performance behavior we decided on was for Helen to respond to Harold's outbursts in a totally new way. In the future, she would maintain unflinching eye contact with him during the entire outburst but say absolutely nothing until the tantrum ended, no matter how long this took. After he finished, she would slowly point her index finger (teacher like) in the direction of his face, and while maintaining eye contact, clearly state, in a normal but assertive tone, "Harold, you can behave at work; you can behave at home." Nothing more, nothing less.

Now that her performance behavior had been defined, a plan using other performance-enhancement techniques, such as role playing and mental rehearsal, was designed and implemented to prepare Helen to carry out her performance behavior confidently and effectively whenever the performance situation occurred.

Harold did not disappoint her. A few days after Helen began rehearsing her new strategy, he had one of his typical outbursts. Flawlessly, she executed her new performance behavior. Harold, totally astonished, stood silently for a moment, then turned and slowly walked into another room. In the weeks that followed, there were only two subsequent outbursts, and each time Helen responded as planned.

Several months later, Helen finished therapy, and I did not hear from her again for six years. When she contacted me, she was beginning divorce proceedings and needed support during this time of life readjustment. Since I had last seen her, she had completed her college degree, found a good job, and had experienced no further problems with Harold's tantrums.

Arousal Control

Successful, elite athletes are able to discover and regulate their optimal state of emotional arousal prior to and during competition.

Strong, seemingly uncontrollable anxiety is one of the several major symptoms that lead many individuals to seek the help of mental health professionals. When this anxiety is associated with a particular life situation, two alternate reactions are typical. One is a tendency to avoid the situation entirely. Betty, as you may recall, avoided air travel for years, depriving herself and her husband of many highly attractive vacation opportunities. Avoidance always has a price, and the price is limiting one's choices and options. People stay with unsatisfactory jobs to avoid the anxiety of a job interview. Others remain in unhappy relationships because they are highly anxious about living alone or starting to date again. Rollo May viewed one of the consequences of anxiety as the person's "shrinking" his or her world to a manageable size.

The second consequence of apparently uncontrollable anxiety is poor performance. Sometimes the individual has no choice and is unable to avoid the anxiety-provoking situation, or he or she bravely chooses to confront it, in spite of anxieties. In either case, avoidance or confrontation, the result is usually discomfort and poor performance. I can remember in second grade being terribly frightened of flash cards. The teacher would randomly call on pupils one at a time to stand up and respond to simple math questions presented on the cards. Her response to errors was always harsh, punitive, and demeaning. Thus, with tense muscles, dry mouth, fast heartbeat, and queasy stomach, I would stand up to answer math questions. Needless to say, with such fear and distractions, I made errors that I would not normally have made, reinforcing the anxiety, which became even greater on future occasions.

There's a paradox to anxiety. Very often the emotion is unintentionally self-inflicted and anticipatory. The individual imagines what he thinks will happen, then reacts emotionally to his own images as if they were real. Then, entering the real-life situation already in this turbulent, emotional state, he is unable to perform well and brings about the very consequences that he feared—truly, a self-fulfilling prophecy.

Athletes have discovered that their best performances occur not when they are totally relaxed, but with an optimum amount of anxiety or arousal. With too little arousal, we are bored, lethargic, and unmotivated. With too much arousal, we are frightened and distracted by our own images, negative prophecies, and somatic disturbances. The optimum level of arousal brings out our best. It wakes us up, makes us vigilant and attentive to the task, makes us care about the outcome, and "gets the juices flowing." Each of us has our own optimum level of arousal for a given task.

Discovering that optimal level of arousal and learning how to regulate it can lead an athlete to successful performances where anxiety had once dominated. For example, Matt, the young figure skater, was so anxious before competitions that he became sick to his stomach. After learning to relax, using the methods that I am about to discuss, his skating improved and he enjoyed his competitions more.

With both athletes and clinical clients, more than 90 percent of the time "arousal regulation" means reducing anxiety. Rarely, although on occasion it does happen, I am asked to help an athlete or client increase the arousal level (energizing) in a performance situation.

Relaxation Training

Teaching clients how to reduce anxiety and be more relaxed in a performance situation is accomplished through several steps of relaxation training and practice. My clients follow this sequence:

1. Relax in my office with my guidance.

2. Relax at home with an audiotape that we make.

3. Relax at home without the tape.

4. Relax with a trigger word or phrase in real-life, low-demand situations.

5. Relax with the trigger word or phrase while mentally rehearsing the performance situation.

6. Relax before and during the performance situation.

At each stage I give the client detailed instructions on how to practice these exercises and skills on a daily basis. Those who are conscientious and carry out the instructions realize appreciable improvements within four to six weeks from our first session.

After explaining the process to the client, we begin our first step with a twenty-minute physical relaxation exercise, an adaptation of Edmund Jacobson's progressive relaxation. During this time, the client is sitting with eyes closed in a comfortable chair. After a preliminary general relaxation suggestion, I instruct him to tense a specific muscle group, such as the left hand, then hold the tension, notice how it feels, then release the tension and relax the same muscles. This is repeated one or two times; then we work on another muscle group. Each time the client's attention is called to how the muscles feel when tense and how they feel when relaxed, to begin teaching the client a sensitivity to his own body so that later, in a real-life situation, he will be able to assess his degree of tension or relaxation and adjust accordingly.

The sequence that I use begins with hands and arms, progresses to scalp and face, neck and shoulders, abdomen, lower back, and finally legs and feet. At the conclusion of the session, the client is instructed to notice how his body feels in this state of deep relaxation: "Notice how your body feels when it is deeply relaxed . . . your body feels heavy and limp . . . your breathing is deep and slow . . .

your heartbeat is slow and steady . . . and your mind is calm and clear." The final suggestion offered is, "Each time you practice relaxation using this tape, you will notice three things. First, you will relax more quickly. Second, you will relax more deeply. And, third, the good feelings of relaxation will remain with you longer and longer after you've finished your practice session." The therapy session concludes with instructions of when and how to do self-relaxation training using the tape, at least once a day for a week.

Depending on the client's progress, the second relaxation training session, mental relaxation, is conducted in a similar fashion one or two weeks later. This procedure is essentially light hypnosis, but for a variety of practical reasons, I have come to prefer the term *relaxation and guided imagery*. During this session, the client may already demonstrate the benefits of his practice with the cassette tape by responding to relaxation suggestions quickly. I monitor galvanic skin response (GSR) with finger electrodes, which give me a rough index of the client's relative state of relaxation throughout the session.

After initial relaxation instructions, which include some of the phrases from the previous session, I suggest that time is slowing down. Shortly after, I suggest a vivid relaxing scene that the client has selected prior to starting the session. My "warm summer's day on a beach by the ocean" scenario has received many favorable reviews. Finally, a trigger word or phrase is introduced, such as, "I am becoming calm and relaxed," that the client can use in real-life situations when this phase of the training is completed. This session is recorded on the backside of the audiocassette tape, and the client is instructed to practice this new recording at least once a day for about two weeks.

Soon after, I instruct the client to engage in six to eight mini-relaxations in the course of everyday life, in settings that are not associated with the performance situation. The mini-relaxation takes one to two minutes. Initially the client practices it while sitting, with eyes closed and few distractions. As the client becomes more skilled, I encourage him to practice with eyes open, standing and sitting and with a variety of visual and auditory distractions. During these sessions, the client quickly becomes relaxed by using the trigger word or phrase associated with relaxation while practicing with the tape. Additionally, I teach him how to relax quickly with deep breathing and mental focusing on his breathing.

The next step is to begin preparing the client to use his newly acquired relaxation skills in the performance situation. The first procedure is to have him begin using the mini-relaxation technique in situations that increasingly approximate his performance situation. For Helen, this might be relaxing at home during the half-hour before Harold returns from work. The second procedure is to incorporate the relaxation practice into a mental rehearsal of his performance behavior, a technique that will be elaborated on later in this chapter.

Preperformance Routines

If the client's performance behavior is one that is likely to be repeated on a regular basis, such as a college student's taking exams, it may be of benefit to help the client develop and practice a preperformance routine: a carefully planned sequence of behaviors designed to prepare the person mentally for the task at hand. The routine becomes familiar and comforting and helps the client to focus attention on simple tasks that are under her control. Such simple routines can be observed in athletes, for example, when a pitcher goes through such a routine before each windup or a basketball player before her free throw. The routine may take a few seconds or several hours, depending on the circumstances.

As a college and graduate student, I discovered that I could regulate my mind-set before major exams by following the same procedure each time. I would complete all of my studying before 11:00 P.M. and attempt to get a good night's rest. Early the next day, I would review highlights of my notes for about a half-hour, emphasizing material that I knew well and avoiding material that was too late to learn. After eating a good breakfast, I would leave my apartment about an hour before the start of the exam, leaving all books, notes, and other associated materials behind. No more studying, no more thinking about the subject matter until the exam began. I would drive to campus, park, walk to the examination room, and claim my chair. Then I would go outdoors and walk, no matter what the weather, returning to the classroom alert, refreshed, and relaxed about five minutes before the start of the exam.

Relaxation training procedure has become a basic building block for most of my athlete and clinical clients who have experienced performance difficulties due to anxiety. Notice that the relaxation response is initially established and practiced without association to the stressful situation. Only after the client has become skilled at self-relaxation do we begin to apply it to the performance situation.

So, for example, I taught Betty how to relax skillfully before beginning to associate the relaxation with her being at an airport or aboard an airplane. Before Helen could practice her new effective, assertive response to Harold's temper outbursts, she would have to attenuate the anxiety that had paralyzed her in the past. The same preparatory process has been used in therapy programs that I've conducted with students overcoming test anxieties, a housewife with a severe spider phobia, an orchestra musician preparing for an important audition, a mother preparing to give a talk at a Parent-Teacher Association meeting, and hundreds of others.

Once the client is freed from the debilitating effects of anxiety, we are ready to employ other appropriate performance-enhancement techniques to their specific situation.

Attention Control

Successful, elite athletes have the ability to develop a precise awareness of what stimuli they need to attend to during a particular game or sport situation. They have the ability to maintain focus on these stimuli and resist all form of distraction, whether from the environment or from within one's self; to regain focus when it has been lost during competition; and to play in the here-and-now without regard to either past or anticipated future events.

A basketball player stands at the free-throw line, just having missed the first of his two shots. As he prepares for his second shot, an unfriendly crowd behind the basket attempts to distract him by waving hundreds of balloons and screaming wildly. For a moment he is aware of the distractions as well as the close score and his having missed his first shot. Then he focuses his attention on the basket and the task at hand. All distractions vanish, and he scores the point.

In any performance situation, there are usually a limited number of things that one must pay attention to in order to perform well. Attention drawn or given to anything else is a distraction that adversely affects performance. The effective college student taking a final calculus exam focuses narrowly on one problem at a time. In this mental state, he is unaware of the sounds of other students, the warm temperature of the room, a car horn outside, mild hunger pangs in his stomach, his previous score on a calculus test, and his goal of getting all A's this quarter. He loses a sense of time, and several hours pass quickly, as if they were only a few minutes. Afterward, he reports that being in this mental state was an enjoyable experience.

By contrast, the unfocused student finds her attention wandering from one distraction to another. She attempts to work on one problem but finds her mind preoccupied with dreadful thoughts of previous problems that she probably missed and how many more might await her on the remainder of the test. She is bothered by the warm temperature of the room, and her attention is easily captured by the sounds of the car horn outside and the other students. She keeps reminding herself that she "better do well" on this test, or she will be in big trouble with the university and with her father.

Once a performance situation has been determined for the client, it needs to be analyzed in detail so that the client has a clear understanding of what she is supposed to be focusing her attention on. This information can often be drawn from the client using interview techniques or having the client walk through the performance behavior, such as the first few minutes of an important job interview, while sharing her stream of consciousness aloud. During the walk-through, the client is encouraged to imagine herself in the actual situation and attempt to think the thoughts and feel the feelings that she would actually experience. Sometimes role playing the situation is effective. Either of these techniques can be effective in identifying distracting, internal thoughts specific to this client.

Resisting Internal Distractions

Once the client is aware of the appropriate objects for her attention, training can begin. In dealing with internal, distracting thoughts, which are often negative and reflect self-doubt, the client's own past strategy is often reported as something like, "I try hard not to think about the previous interviews in which I screwed up." At that point, I usually demonstrate the ineffectiveness of negative suggestions by telling the client at that moment to think about anything in the universe except "a pink-and-blue-striped whale. Do not think about a pink-and-blue-striped whale. Now what image has come to mind?"

This usually elicits an insightful smile. "Let's try this again, but we'll do it differently. Picture an elephant in your mind. See this image as clearly and as vividly as you can. Now, when I tell you to think about anything except the pink-and-blue-striped whale, ignore me by focusing intensively on your image of the elephant. Notice how much easier it is to ignore a negative suggestion when it's replaced by a strong positive suggestion." In a real-life situation, the strong, positive image may be elicited by cue words or positive affirmations, both discussed in the next section.

We discuss the concept that we can choose what we think about at any moment. As an illustration, I ask the client to think about a scene from a pleasant vacation, then to think about a problem related to work. I ask him to close his eyes and then, under my direction, alternately think about the vacation and then think about the work problem. After a few moments, I ask him to do this while I remain silent. Then, finally, I ask him to think so powerfully about the vacation for a few minutes that there is no room in his consciousness for any other thoughts. After a few moments, I present the conflicting thoughts about the work problem in a low voice while instructing him to block me out by continuing to focus intensively on the vacation scene. Most clients are able to do this with some degree of success even on their first attempt. Most believe that they will improve this ability to control their own thoughts if they practice the exercise on a regular basis.

In golf, there is more thinking time than in most other sports; often there are several minutes between shots. Golfers who dwell on self-doubt and past mistakes lose their concentration. Learning to select and focus attention on a simple, clear, positive image helps to block out such distractions.

Resisting External Distractions

For learning the selective attention that is necessary for blocking out distractions from the external environment, I often use the following exercise in guided imagery, inspired by Robert Nideffer's concepts of broad versus narrow external focus of attention. The client relaxes with his eyes closed for a short period of time. I then ask the person to imagine as vividly as possible the following scene:

> You are sitting on the first floor, near the center of a very large theater. It's a full house, and all of the seats are occupied. You can feel the cushion of the theater seat beneath you, and your arms resting comfortably on the armrests. As you begin to look around this large auditorium, you notice that the only source of light is a single light bulb hanging from a cord in the center of the ceiling. The light is dim but sufficient for you to see the entire room. On the ceiling, you can discern beautiful artwork, but faintly illuminated, and a crystal chandelier, faintly illuminated. As you look around the audience, you can see people in all of the seats, but in shades of gray. On the

stage in front of you is a human figure, but the light is so faint that you're unable to distinguish whether it's a man, a woman, or a child, the person's clothing, or the facial expression. Yes, you can see everything in this large room, but everything is faintly illuminated.

Now, I'd like you to imagine that someone has taken the light bulb and placed it on the balcony, in a tube, with a mirror at the rear and a lens at the front. The person has created a spotlight, and it's shining brightly on the figure in the middle of the stage. Now you can very clearly see this brightly illuminated figure; you can distinguish whether it's a man, a woman, or a child. You can see the style and the bright colors of the clothing and even discern the facial expression. But as you look around the auditorium, you now notice that everything else has receded into darkness. You can no longer see the artwork on the ceiling, only darkness. You can no longer see the crystal chandelier, only darkness. And you can no longer see the people in the audience, only darkness. You can see the figure on the stage very vividly, but everything else has faded into darkness.

As you can see from this example, the same amount of light from the light bulb can be used in two different ways. It can be used in a wide mode, in which it shines on everything, but only faintly. Or it can be used in a narrow mode, in which the same amount of light is highly focused and illuminates one aspect of the environment very brightly, but the rest fades into darkness. The light can be switched back and forth between the two modes. Now imagine the light and what you see while it's in the wide mode . . . now in the narrow mode . . . back to the wide mode . . . the narrow. Now let that scene fade away and simply feel your relaxation.

Your mind is very much like that light bulb. Sometimes it functions in a wide mode, sometimes in a narrow mode. You already do this in everyday life. However, you can become even better at this with practice. In order to perform well in performance situations, it is important for you to be able to regulate your mode of attention and have control over it. Let's go back to the theater, and just using your mind, without the light bulb, picture the theater in a wide mode . . . now a narrow mode . . . wide mode . . . narrow mode. Let the scene fade away and feel the relaxation in your body.

At this point I insert an exercise that is tailored to the individual client's performance situation. Following is an example from my work with a trial attorney who experienced high performance anxiety in the courtroom, before and while he was presenting opening arguments to the judge:

Now imagine yourself in a courtroom, a typical one, or an actual courtroom in which you frequently practice. It's a few moments before you are to present an opening argument to the judge. You are well prepared and have a clear outline of your major points in your head. You are aware of your total courtroom environment: the high ceiling, the furniture, decorations on the walls, the jury, other attorneys. You hear the familiar sounds of the courtroom just before the court is called to order. Now, a few minutes later, it's time for you to present your opening argument to the judge. You approach the bench and go into a narrow focus. You are keenly aware of the judge to whom you are about to present. You are aware of your body and your mind, which is calm and clear. There is a calm awareness of your major points and your opening words that you are about to speak. All else has faded away, as if in darkness. You are totally and completely focused on the judge, yourself, and the task at hand. You begin to speak, with confidence and clarity. Now slowly allow the scene to fade away.

After doing the above exercise, which is tape-recorded for the client's home practice, I guide the client through a one-minute attention-focusing exercise that he is encouraged to practice after playing the tape and six or seven times a day, in a variety of environments:

Sitting comfortably, as you are now, select an object in your environment that is in front of you, such as the coffee mug on the table. Look at the coffee mug with a narrow mode of focus. Pretend that your eyes are laser beams and that you're burning a hole through it. About ten to fifteen seconds. Now switch to a wide mode, without moving your eyes or head; just using your mind, keep staring at the mug, but become aware of other things within your view: the coffee table, the color and texture of the carpet, the chairs, pictures on the wall. Now back to the narrow mode . . . wide mode . . . narrow mode. Now switch back and forth a few times, without my coaching. . . . Okay, that's fine; you may stop now.

Blocking Out Distractions

In order to help Betty relax while on an airplane, it was important for her to be able to block out thoughts that were counterproductive and anxiety producing. She had a long list of skillfully developed disaster scenarios that included midair collisions, a wing falling off the aircraft, and multiple engine failures. As with the "Don't think about a pink-and-blue-striped whale exercise," we created a strong, positive image of an airplane, built to endure one hundred times the stress that it would ever experience, and with electronic navigation and collision devices. In practice sessions, Betty alternated between her disaster images and the alternative that I had provided for her. She learned to image the strong airplane so vividly that she was able to block out the frightening images.

Using variations of these techniques, Helen was able to focus on her new, assertive responses to Harold's temper tantrums and block out her previous self-doubting thoughts, as well as the external distractions that Harold would surely provide. Similar benefits were achieved by the distracted student and the courtroom attorney.

Self-Talk

> Successful, elite athletes are able to manage self-confidence and challenges in a positive, constructive manner through healthy habits of self-talk. Sometimes self-talk is based on cognitive-behavioral strategies for reframing a situation or simply a cue word selected to elicit specific thoughts, feelings, and behaviors.

Fear and avoidance of a performance situation are often perpetuated by the client through habitual, negative, defeatist self-talk. Betty, for example, said for many years, both aloud and to herself, "I'm frightened to death of riding in an airplane." Such self-talk reinforces a negative, ineffective self-concept and evokes images and emotions that reinforce the fear. Sometimes the self-talk transcends a specific situation and leads to a global, self-deprecating statement, such as "I just can't do anything right." Often the client is unaware of the strength, frequency, and negativity of these statements. Since self-talk mediates images, emotions, and behavior, it is important to teach the client to develop more effective self-talk habits.

Revising Negative Self-Talk: "Becoming Your Own Best Friend"

The first step in this process is making the client aware of his negative self-talk and its consequences. In my therapy sessions, I listen carefully for such utterances. The college calculus student who is easily distracted during tests says, "I'm a terrible student." I request an instant replay: "Did you hear what you just said? Please repeat it for me."

Many times the client is unable to do so. If he cannot, I will repeat it for him. Then I ask several thought-provoking questions, such as, "How does this statement make you feel? To what extent does it motivate you to improve? How would you feel if a friend said that to you? Are there other negative statements that you say to yourself?" Typically the answers are predictable: "The statement makes me feel lousy. It doesn't motivate me. It makes me feel like quitting school. My feelings would be hurt if a friend said that to me. Yeah, I'm always putting myself down."

Then I intervene: "Since you can say anything you want to yourself, it doesn't make sense to me that you would choose to say things that make you feel bad, discourage you, and hurt your own feelings. Why not say something that will make you feel good and motivate you toward achieving your goals? What could you say that would accomplish that and also be true?"

After some discussion, the two of us settle on the statement: "Although school is difficult at times, I love it and learning. As I learn how to concentrate effectively, I will overcome the barrier that has frustrated me in taking tests." I ask the client to write this affirmative statement on an index card and carry it with her for a few weeks. Each time she catches herself beginning to think, "I am a terrible student," she is to stop the thought as quickly as possible and then read the alternative message from the card.

To extend the learning from this exercise in the therapy session to the client's everyday life, I will ask the client to carry a blank card with her at all times and to write down each instance of negative self-talk. Then, on her own or in session with me, she is instructed to rewrite each message as she wishes her "best friend" would speak to her: "You're the only one you'll ever have to live with twenty-four hours a day for your entire life, so become your own best friend!"

Positive Affirmations

A slight variation of the technique is the use of positive affirmations. As the client is preparing for performance behavior in a performance situation, the anticipated pressure of the situation may begin to evoke negative images and thoughts. To counter this in advance, part of the preparation may include generating several positive affirmations that the client will practice associating with the anticipated event. Good positive affirmations are usually short "I" statements that the client believes to be true. They work best when stated in the present tense and cannot be proved wrong, even if the outcome of the situation turns out to be unfavorable. Usually I help the client to generate three positive affirmations for a situation. They are written on a small index card and carried at all times until memorized.

For example, Helen prepares herself for behaving in an assertive manner in response to Harold's next outburst. She reaches into her purse and pulls out the index card with these words written on it:

I am strong.

I am assertive.

I have a plan.

Upon reading these words, she invokes in herself positive thoughts, feelings, and images that will serve her well when she applies her new behavior to the real-life situation.

Cue Words or Phrases

Cue words or phrases are similar to positive affirmations except that they are associated with a highly specific situation and intended to evoke a specific, practiced response. They have already been referred to as part of the earlier discussions of relaxation training and attention focusing. The cue word is often the bridge between the training experience and using the new skill in a real-life situation.

For example, in the relaxation training procedure that I described above, the cue phrase, "I am becoming calm and relaxed," was used to evoke the relaxation response in real-life situations when the client started to feel anxious. The college student and courtroom attorney learned to block out the distractions that had plagued them in the past by learning to say or think the word "focus" whenever their attention began to drift. Betty successfully blocked the upsetting airplane disaster images from her mind with the words "strong, powerful airplane," which came to evoke that image instead.

Emotional Control

Successful, elite athletes are able to control strong emotions—anger, elation, or despondency—when they interfere with performance. These emotional states frequently accompany mistakes and errors or sometimes performing above one's expectations.

Although closely related to anxiety or arousal control, and attention focusing, emotional control represents a unique combination of several of the other mental skills. Often an athlete's anger flares up suddenly in reaction to an unexpected event, such as missing an easy shot in golf, an official's "unfair" call, or an opponent's tormenting behavior. The sudden, powerful emotion compels attention away from appropriate stimuli, and concentration is lost. Visceral changes add to the distraction, and muscle tension prevents smooth, coordinated behavior. Finally, there is a tendency toward expressive, aggressive behavior against the object of the anger. Behaviors that express the emotion directly may violate the rules of the game and lead to a penalty or, at the very least, cause athletes to lose concentration. It is not an unusual practice for athletes to attempt to inflame their opponents deliberately in order to make them lose their cool.

Successful, elite athletes remain centered and focused and are rarely disrupted by these strong feelings. When they experience anger, they have the skills for diminishing it quickly and effectively. Usually this is accomplished by maintaining focus on the task at hand, on things that can be controlled, and appropriate self-talk with statements such as, "Just let it go; plan your next action."

In everyday life, some clients have difficulty in managing anger, often evoked by their own imperfections or the behaviors of others. If this is to be addressed in the therapy by using these performance-enhancement techniques, then we need to analyze and plan for appropriate responses to anger situations and prepare for them. For the individual client, the case history and interview can usually identify specific hot spots: events, persons, and situations where the sudden anger is likely to occur. Once they are identified, a specific set of appropriate behaviors becomes the therapeutic goal. The behaviors may then be role-played with the therapist or others, associated with cue words, and practiced during mental rehearsal. The most important step is helping the client to become sensitive to the first signs of his rising anger and to use the appropriate mental tools before the anger becomes too great.

Jim, a hard-working forty-two-year-old husband and father of two teenaged boys, became easily enraged whenever his older son failed to perform his household chores. Jim's perception was that the boy just didn't care and was unappreciative of the father's hard work and good example that he set. When he would discover such negligence on the part of the son, it was usually shortly after arriving home from a hard day at work, when he was tired and irritable. Typically he would yell loudly at the son, say extremely cruel things about the boy's character, and threaten to throw him out of the house. Jim was not a cruel man by nature. After he cooled down, he would feel very guilty and try to make it up to his son by being unusually kind and solicitous, a behavior that he knew was inappropriate and not beneficial to the boy.

After some discussion in our sessions, Jim decided that the way he would like to act in this situation would be to "talk himself out of an immediate reaction" and later talk to his son in a businesslike way. The calming self-talk that he chose was the phrase, "It's not that bad; we can deal with this later." He decided to simply tell the son that he had a problem that they needed to talk about in a little while, after he changed his clothing and settled down from work. If he felt the anger becoming too strong and approaching loss of control, he would walk around the block.

We role-played this situation in therapy several times with many variations and later made a mental rehearsal tape for Jim to practice with at home. Within several weeks Jim reported a high degree of success in controlling his anger using this technique. He also discovered that the son was much less defensive and more cooperative when he was talked to in a businesslike manner.

The last concept in this section, managing strong, positive emotions such as elation, seems paradoxical. After all, success is what we're striving for. The athlete who experiences an unexpected success may lose her focus due to her sudden excitement or may worry that more will be expected of her now and that she may not be able to live up to these new expectations. Similarly, the person who receives an unexpected commendation or promotion may experience elation that leads to subsequent anxiety and self-doubt. Once again, the most effective strategy for coping with this type of situation is to help the client focus on immediate, here-and-now tasks over which she has some degree of control.

Mental Imagery

Successful, elite athletes are able to imagine themselves performing specific behaviors at a high level of excellence, using multiple sensory modalities: mentally rehearsing situations and performances in advance and dealing with errors and poor performances through mental imagery correction rather than reliving the mistake mentally.

Throughout this chapter I have made frequent references to mental images that the client creates and then responds to as if they were real. We have already dealt with alternate methods for helping the client develop an awareness of her images, as well as the tools for altering, blocking, and controlling these mental images when necessary. In this final section, to put it all together, we look at one of the most powerful techniques that elite, successful athletes use in preparation for high levels of performance behavior in performance situations: mental rehearsal.

Let us assume that you have made effective use of the performance-enhancement tools in preparing your client to deal effectively with a particular situation. You have assessed the person's motivation, set appropriate goals and developed a plan for achieving them, and taught the client techniques for managing anxiety and focusing her attention appropriately. Finally, your client has learned to self-regulate images, thoughts, and emotions through the use of cue words. These skills may have been acquired individually, but before they will be fully effective, it is necessary to integrate them into a realistic scenario that the client can use in final preparation.

Mental rehearsal is the creation and use of an obtainable fantasy. Having previously collected detailed information about the performance situation from the client, you now construct a positive, realistic walk-through scenario and guide the client through it in imagery. You incorporate into the images specific challenges that the client must deal with, as well as all of the previous techniques that you have taught.

Approximately two weeks before Betty's scheduled flight to San Francisco, we made a mental rehearsal tape of the anticipated events. Betty sat with her eyes closed in the comfortable chair that had now become familiar to her. Her GSR was monitored so that I could note any particular places where her anxiety increased. The following script is a condensation of the actual script, which contained more detailed descriptions and more repetition. As with other therapeutic applications of mental imagery, it is important that images be very detailed and that multiple sensory modalities be used. After giving Betty a few moments to relax herself, I began.

I'd like you to imagine the scenes that are to follow as clearly and as vividly as you possibly can. Experience the scene with all of your senses: seeing, hearing, tasting, smell, and touching. If at any time you find yourself becoming anxious, reduce your anxiety, as you've been doing successfully, with the thoughts, "I am becoming calm and relaxed." If any troublesome images about an airplane enter your mind, you now know that you can replace them with a positive image, using the words "strong, powerful airplane." So let's begin.

After walking through a detailed description of her evening and morning routines, travel to airport, check-in, breakfast, and waiting at the boarding gate (which were on Betty's tape) we fast-forward to boarding the plane:

After sitting for fifteen minutes at the gate, you hear over the loudspeaker, "Passengers are now boarding Flight Number 309 for San Francisco at Gate 12." You can begin to feel your heart pounding as you rise and begin walking. Your stomach feels a bit queasy, but you quickly say to yourself, "I am becoming calm and relaxed." The tension immediately begins to subside, and you now relax even further by imagining yourself holding your new granddaughter. As you leave the walkway and enter the airplane, again tension rises, but again you are able to reduce it by controlling your thoughts. This time you decide to focus your attention on the pleasant smiles and greeting of the flight crew. You and Ralph find your seats, stow your overhead baggage, and sit down. Your seat feels comfortable, and as you fasten your seatbelt, the "snap" sound reminds you of the seatbelt in your car and the exciting feeling of leaving for a vacation by car. Finally, all passengers are seated. The doors are closed and the engines start. The plane taxies slowly toward the runway. . . .

[Now fast-forward to the end of the flight.] Below the airplane's wing you can now see the cars and houses becoming larger and larger as the plane descends and approaches the airport. Finally, you can see the black tarmac of the runway. There is a loud thump as the wheels strike the ground, and you hear the rising sound of the engines as the plane brakes hard. You feel the tug of your seatbelt as the plane slows. Then it's over. The plane taxies slowly toward the terminal. Suddenly you feel a rush of emotion and excitement; your heart is beating rapidly, but it's a good feeling, a wonderful feeling of jubilation. In a few moments, you'll be holding your infant granddaughter in your arms.

But right now you feel like a conquering hero. You have successfully overcome your fear of flying by using the mental skills that you've practiced so diligently during the past six weeks.

And just as she imagined it, six weeks after she walked into my office, Betty did it.

———————

Applying the techniques of sport psychology to your clinical clients is an excellent bridge between the practice that you used to have and the future practice that you envisioned in Chapter One. As you become increasingly comfortable and proficient in the use of these techniques, you'll be ready to seek new clients: those who participate in sports and specifically seek the services of a sport psychologist.

5

Introduction to Working with Athletes

Now that you've been developing sport psychology skills with clinical clients, you're ready to begin applying these skills to athletes. In some ways, this will be easier, but in other ways more difficult. In this chapter, we'll look at how working with athletes is different from working with your clinical clientele.

Athletes may come to you for two different types of services. First, like everyone else, athletes have life adjustment difficulties and psychological disorders, with a consequent need for counseling and psychotherapy. You are already trained to provide these services and will be an even more effective provider as you come to understand the special characteristics of athletes and the environments in which they function. The second reason that athletes will come to you is for specific mental skills training in order to improve their performances in competition. Since you will be working with the whole person, you may be providing both types of service to a single individual.

In my own experience with athletes, one of these services usually predominates, and the other is secondary. Sometimes our focus is primarily clinical and counseling, and performance enhancement is secondary. With other athletes, this may be reversed. This decision is made on the basis of the client's presenting problem, my professional assessment and recommendations, and mutual discussion and goal setting with the client. The goals we establish, usually during the first or second session, reflect the degree to which the emphasis of our work will be on clinical and counseling work versus performance enhancement. As our work together progresses, these initial decisions may be modified and appropriately adjusted.

The distinction between clinical and counseling work and performance enhancement is relevant to us as professionals, to ensure that we practice techniques that are within the limits of our competence and training. In the real worlds of the client and the helping relationship, this distinction is less important. In the end we, as therapists working with whole people, aim to help clients discover and use their resources in order to deal more effectively with their life situations.

Before beginning to focus on working with athletes, let's look at some of the ways in which this will be different from your clinical work.

A CONTINUUM OF COMMITMENT

Athletes may be described or categorized in many different ways: by sport, age, gender, and level of achievement or proficiency. One of the most relevant, from the perspective of the sport psychologist, is the degree of commitment that the athlete has to his or her sport. A continuum of commitment that I have found to be useful looks like this: casual participant, to recreational athlete, to serious recreational athlete, to committed recreational athlete, to elite athlete. Each progressive level represents an increase in the importance that sport plays in the life of the individual. Generally, as we go up the scale, the person is devoting more time, effort, and resources to the sport and is expecting more in return in terms of performance, achievement, and recognition. The higher the level, the higher the goals that the person has set.

In addition to reflecting the importance of sport in the person's life, the continuum also reflects a developmental sequence. Most elite athletes have progressed through all of the stages, and probably rather quickly. Other athletes reach a certain level and do not go beyond, due to their choice or to limitations of ability and life circumstances. It is not unusual for an athlete to move up or down the continuum as sports interest and other life factors change.

The same progression as the steps in this continuum will be helpful for you in developing and applying your performance-enhancement skills. Start by working with serious recreational athletes. They have probably not worked on their mental skills in an organized fashion, and doing an assessment and intervention with them will be easier than with the more committed and elite athletes. As you hone your skills, seek and accept the challenges of working with higher-level athletes.

Obviously this advice is irrelevant when you are applying your clinical and counseling skills. Rather than using this continuum, your established areas of clinical expertise and competence will determine the appropriateness of a particular client, independent of whether the person is an athlete.

The Casual Participant

The continuum begins with the casual participant, who probably would not think to use the label "athlete" in describing her involvement in sports. The casual participant plays for fun and is not particularly concerned about her level of proficiency, improvement, and win-loss record. Her participation is likely to be sporadic and motivated by social as well as other needs that are not particularly sports related. Playing basketball in a neighbor's back yard several times each summer is an example. This category can encompass the person who has just begun jogging, exercising at the gym, playing some tennis or golf, and all without an intense commitment or specific goals.

The casual participant gives little thought to the sport except while actually playing it. Nevertheless, every casual participant has the potential for becoming a more serious athlete. Often people begin playing a sport casually and discover satisfactions and benefits that result in their becoming more serious and committed to their

sport. Judy, for example, first played volleyball only at company pic-
nics, but she enjoyed the game and thought it might help her to get
back in shape. Now she plays two evenings a week in a league and
has become quite competitive.

Some of your clinical clients may be casual participants in sport
or exercise and may benefit physically and mentally from an increased level of participation. Your interest and encouragement can
be a catalyst in helping them go through this transition. Only last
week, Beth, one of my clients who, at my suggestion, began regular
jogging on a treadmill to reduce depression, entered my office with
a large grin. She had completed a ten-kilometer race the day before,
her first athletic competition since mandatory physical education
classes in high school. This accomplishment had a marvelous effect
on her self-esteem and motivated her to train for another race and
a faster time.

The Recreational Athlete

The next step in the continuum, recreational athletes generally participate in their sport on a regular basis. If the activity is solitary,
such as jogging, they have usually made a self-commitment to run
on certain days or to run at least a predetermined number of days
each week. If the sport is a team or organized sport, they sign up and
commit to playing and practicing on a regularly scheduled basis.
However, the commitment is to participation rather than performance. The benefits that they experience come through the activity, not the performance outcome.

Many runners and golfers I have known love their sport and participate regularly, but their enjoyment remains quite independent
of how well they've done. They are keenly aware of the noncom-
petitive benefits of participation such as health and fitness, effective stress management, and enjoying friends.

Many athletes pass through this stage on the way to becoming
more committed and more serious about their sport, and many committed and elite athletes I've known long to return to this mode of
participation. Particularly middle-aged men and women who have

achieved at high levels that they can no longer sustain wish to return to this stage, where they can enjoy their sport again without worrying about their performance. Such athletes, as well as those whose performances have decreased due to injury and time demands from their other life commitments, can benefit from counseling in making this adjustment.

The Serious Recreational Athlete

Serious recreational athletes care about their performance and are highly motivated to do well. Their scores, times, finishing places, improvements, and win-loss records are important because they have chosen to make them important. In reality, there may be no major real life consequences to successful high achievement. Regardless of performance, these athletes are likely to continue working at the same job, live in the same house, and so forth. Nevertheless, they care about how they're doing and think about their sport a great deal even when they're not actively playing, as well as off-season.

Playing well and improving is necessary for this type of athlete to have fun. Their actual quality of performance, from an objective point of view, is irrelevant. For example, I work with equally serious recreational golfers who play "zero handicap" golf and others who have a handicap of fifteen or more. It's their attitude toward their sport, not their level of performance, that makes them serious athletes. Although they devote significant resources toward their sport participation and improvement, sport remains secondary to other important aspects of their lives, such as family and career.

The Committed Athlete

Committed athletes live for their sport. Goal oriented and committed to the work ethic, they have already achieved at a high level and have even higher aspirations for the future. They devote considerable time and money in order to develop their sport abilities. Often career, school, and sometimes even friends and family are secondary to their sport development. For committed athletes, there is no off-season. They devote so much of their time to their sport that they may have few other interests or friends outside of their sport. Indeed, they usually have dreams and aspirations that achieving their high-level sports goals—winning a university scholarship, making All-American, being drafted by a professional team, winning a gold medal at the Olympics—will lead to major changes in their life.

Committed athletes' love of their sport participation is rarely unconditional. Their enjoyment and satisfaction are usually dependent on satisfactory performances so they are vulnerable to becoming quite upset with themselves when they have gone through a streak of disappointing performances.

Although this category of athlete is high on the continuum, you may be surprised to discover some very young athletes who have already adopted this lifestyle. We see examples of this in youth sports such as gymnastics, tennis, figure skating, swimming, and ice hockey. This degree of commitment in young athletes raises questions with respect to healthy physical, psychological, and social development, which will be addressed later in this book.

The Elite Athlete

Elite athletes are committed athletes who have succeeded. Their natural talent, diligence, and commitment to their sport have led to high levels of achievement for which they have been recognized. After years and years of struggle and sacrifice, their recognition often has a sudden onset, occasioned by winning a tournament or an Olympic medal, for example.

Although the concerns of elite athletes are similar to those of committed athletes, their life circumstances and pressures are considerably different. In addition to the pressure to perform consistently at higher and higher levels of competition, they also have to deal with new issues, such as sudden fame, wealth, media, and managers.

ATHLETES AS CLIENTS

In working with casual participants, athletes at the beginning of the continuum, you will probably find few differences from your usual clients. As you progress up the continuum in the direction of elite athletes, you will discover more and more differences, in both the nature of these clients and your manner of working with them. These differences will probably be least significant in clinical and counseling work and most significant when your work is performance enhancement. Let's look at some of the differences that you can expect.

Motivation

On the average, the more serious the athlete is, the more likely he is to be highly motivated, optimistic, respectful, goal oriented, result seeking, positive, willing to take direction, expectant of homework, compliant with homework assignments, self-monitoring, and hard working. Not bad! He is, however, also likely to be self-focused, narrow in interests, limited in nonsport interests and skills, and emotionally and socially underdeveloped. These attributes are more likely to be found in relatively young elite athletes who have overspecialized in developing their sport skills, to the neglect of other life skills.

Performance Behaviors in Demanding Situations

Compared to working with your clinical clients, selecting performance behaviors in demanding situations will be quite easy. With your clinical clients, this often takes considerable skill and effort. In some cases, as I discussed in the previous chapter, the client's motivation and a host of other issues have to be considered. Remember Helen, for example, where I had to collect case information and process it before selecting the performance behavior as "an assertive response to Harold's tantrums."

With regard to performance enhancement, most athletes will come to you with these matters already defined. The golfer, for example, wants help in being able to relax and forget about the last shot that she messed up. The basketball player wants to improve his free-throw percentage by improving his concentration. Although things rarely turn out as simple as they appear initially, it will be considerably easier, in most instances when you're working with athletes, to define performance behaviors in demanding situations.

Methods for Improving Performance Behavior

The methods for achieving the desirable outcomes are much more restricted in sports than in everyday life situations due to the rules, limited and defined resources, and the conventions of the sport. In working with Helen, I had many potential strategies available for developing a more effective behavior in response to Harold's temper tantrums. I chose a specific assertive response. If it had not worked, I would have encouraged Helen to consider other alternatives, and even creative behaviors, such as leaving the room whenever Harold became verbally abusive, or leaving the house for an hour, or even squirting him with a water pistol. Within the scope of what is legal and ethical, literally hundreds of alternative behaviors might have been considered.

This is not true when working with an athlete's performance. In most sports, there are restrictions with regard to the range of behaviors that are permitted, the space where the athlete is required to be (or prohibited from being), and time limits within which performance behavior must occur. The basketball free-throw shooter, for example, must remain within certain spatial boundaries, has ten seconds to begin the shot, and is not permitted many behaviors that would be available in everyday life, including an extra chance, if needed, or kicking the ball.

Clarity of Results

Clinical clients present with problems that are usually complex and beyond direct control of either the client or therapist, so it is often difficult to evaluate the results of therapy. The client who overcomes performance anxiety and improves her interview skills may still not get the desired job. The father who overcomes his previous insensitivities and learns to listen more to his son with a nonjudgmental attitude may still remain alienated from his son, who is currently focused on other priorities.

In clinical work, we have learned to accept the ambiguous relationship between the quality of our work and the client outcome.

Because of complexities and varied client motivation, our best-quality work may result in mediocre results or even failure. Fortuitously, there are times when our efforts are associated with favorable client outcome. Seasoned clinicians learn to live with this situation. Since outcomes in the real world are typically beyond the control of either client or therapist, therapeutic goals often are phrased in subjective, process terms such as "feeling better about myself."

When working with athletes' performance behaviors, there appears, correctly or not, to be a stronger connection between the quality of our efforts and the client's results. Since the athletes who seek help are usually highly motivated, they are likely to carry out suggestions that you give them. The environments in which they perform, unlike everyday life situations, are highly controlled—at times almost as well as a laboratory experiment. They have not come to you to "feel better" but for highly specific performance results. Correctly or not, they are likely to evaluate themselves and you in terms of measured results. It's important, therefore, to clarify expectations at the beginning of your work and explain that psychological skills, like athletic skills, take a long time to master, especially under stressful conditions.

Moments of Truth

With clinical clients, life situations tend to evolve over a longer period of time and there are few moments of truth in which results are clear, final, and lasting. Most real-life situations are interactive and continuous. The mother attempting to modify her behavior to improve a relationship with her adolescent daughter may have many occasions in which to try out a variety of behaviors and approaches. This is a long-term process of continuous adjustment that may play out over a period of many years.

For athletes, however, there are usually situations that are important and have a finality to them. A high school senior track star runs poorly in a district meet and is eliminated from going on to the state finals. Her season, and maybe her high school career, come to an abrupt end, as does her opportunity for a college scholarship. In the final game of the season, a college football kicker, in front of television cameras and ninety thousand fans, misses an easy field goal attempt during the final seconds of the game, and his team loses. As a result, the team loses the conference championship and a preferred bowl bid. These are the moments of truth that most athletes have to face.

Maintaining Professional Boundaries

Maintaining professional boundaries may be more difficult with athlete clients than clinical clients. Especially when you're doing performance enhancement, you may meet with your client outside your office, at the practice field or competition site. Most athletes are accustomed to some degree of fraternization with their teammates, coaches, team owners, sponsors, and medical professionals. Since you may be perceived more like a coach or teacher than a psychotherapist (correctly at times), you may occasionally receive invitations for social contact that would be totally inappropriate from a clinical client. Your declining all such invitations may be interpreted by your athlete client as not caring or being too distant. Yet accepting such invitations without careful consideration may compromise your working relationship.

I deal with these situations judiciously. If I can attend a social event without compromising my professional relationship with the client, especially if the occasion is sports or team related, I may do so. But if there is any doubt, I prefer to err on the side of caution and decline the invitation. I acknowledge that I may have a friendly relationship with my athlete client, but I will not risk jeopardizing my effectiveness as a professional by permitting our relationship to become a friendship.

Because many of the athletes that you work with will be personable, upbeat, and mentally healthy, you may find them likable and easy to identify with. Unlike with your clinical clients, you will probably come to witness some of their moments of truth firsthand by attending events or watching them on television. Your own emotions may run high when you sit in the stands watching helplessly as "your" young figure skater falls twice during her program and finishes last, or when you watch the basketball player you've been working with all season set a career high and be awarded "player of the game." These feelings may be even amplified when you work with athletes in high-risk sports such as auto racing. Your emotions may also be triggered by media coverage and commentary that you perceive as unfair. Within this category, sports talk radio can be especially inflammatory.

Sports are about emotion, so expect and prepare yourself for strong emotional experiences. Because you know and care about your athlete clients, your emotional reactions to their successes and failures may be unusually powerful. You handle these feelings in the same way in which you learned to handle this with your clinical clients: by maintaining a professional perspective. As much as you may care, you must be constantly aware of the boundary between you and your client. The experience is theirs, not yours. The success and failure are theirs, not yours. You are a consultant. You will always maintain a professional self-concept that is based on the quality of your work, measured by the standards of your profession, not by the performances of your clients. You learn and improve through your clients' performances, but you are reticent to accept credit for their success or blame for their failures.

Client Confidentiality

Closely related to this issue of boundaries is that of confidentiality. If you attend one of your sport client's competitions, he may introduce you freely and proudly as his "sport psychologist." In other cases, the person may have a strong preference for confidentiality. In the past few years, for example, I have worked with several well-known professional athletes who have sought my services without the knowledge of their team management. Their belief was that the team and the media's knowledge of their working with a sport psychologist would be detrimental to them.

With my clinical background, I automatically assume that the relationship with my athlete client is a confidential one, no different from that which I have with my clinical clients. During the first session, this issue and its implications should be discussed with the client so that you may be aware of any confidentiality concerns that the person may have. Usually I ask for written permission to communicate with the athlete's coach so that I can learn more about the athlete as well as work cooperatively with the coach. Most of the time, the athlete is pleased to grant this permission. If the person is reticent, we discuss the issue, and I abide by the client's decision.

If it is helpful for me to observe the client in practice or competition, we discuss the implications of this in advance. At smaller, local competitions, as in figure skating, I advise my client that I am recognizable by most of the coaches and many of the competitors, so if I interact with the client in this environment, our interaction is likely to be observed and interpreted as my working with him or her professionally. Many of the athletes I work with are quite comfortable with this situation; others are not. In either case, this issue is not left to chance and always discussed with the client in advance.

Even when a client initially comes to me for learning performance-enhancement skills and my primary role is that of educator or consultant, I nevertheless remain cautious about maintaining professional boundaries and respecting confidentially. One never knows in advance when the relationship might expand to include elements of counseling and psychotherapy.

Having summarized some of the ways in which athletes and working with athletes may differ from your usual clinical work, let's move on. Next, we focus more specifically on recreational athletes' needs, and the ways in which sport psychology can be beneficial to them.

6

Working with Recreational Athletes

Sport is not a required course in life. Recreational athletes know that and choose to participate because they believe their participation in sport makes their life better. The number one reason that recreational athletes give for their sport participation is "having fun," but this has different meaning for different athletes. For some it means being outdoors, or becoming fit and healthy. For others it means improving skills, managing stress more effectively, or socializing with friends.

THE NEED FOR BALANCE

Nothing comes without a price, and the benefits of athletic participation come with both costs and potential problems. Each moment spent in sport is a moment taken away from another life activity. Each dollar spent on sport is a dollar unavailable for other purposes. Fatigue, injury, frustration, increased stress, disappointments, and lowered self-esteem may be experienced and overcome or may become a chronic aspect of the recreational athlete's life.

Recreational athletes need to maintain a balance between the benefits of sport participation and the costs and problems that come with the package. They strive to maintain balance among their life priorities: self, family, career, friends, and future. Sometimes sport interferes with life; sometimes life interferes with sport. When

balance is achieved, the recreational athlete's sport should contribute to her overall life enjoyment. Imbalance leads to unhap-
piness, conflict, and frustration. Your understanding and being
sensitive to these concerns will enable you to be a more effective
therapist with your clinical clients who also happen to be recreational athletes, as well as with recreational athletes who are referred to you as a sport psychologist.

To address these issues in my own work with athletes, part of my
intake assessment includes two important questions: "What do you
expect to experience through your sport participation?" and, "To
what extent are you having these experiences?" I ask the second
question periodically throughout our work together.

These two questions have been formatted for quantitative
responses and comprise a brief questionnaire that I devised and refer
to as the Ohio Sport Satisfaction Index (OSSI). Although usually
administered by itself, it also comprises the first two pages of the
Mental Skills Assessment Form (MSAF), contained in the Appendix. During the past few years, I have administered the OSSI to
hundreds of athletes, as well as to the parents and coaches of young
athletes.

The data are very clear about why athletes participate in sports.
"Having fun" is the number one reason, chosen by well over 90 percent of all subjects who have taken the OSSI, regardless of sport,
age, gender, or ability level. Of equal significance, parents and
coaches of young athletes also rate "having fun" as the most important experience they want their children and charges to have
through their sport participation.

In my individual work with athletes, imbalance is often reflected
in low scores on the "having fun" item on the second page of the
OSSI. This is a red flag and an appropriate point of departure for
further assessment. What is preventing the athlete from having fun?
A wide variety of answers may be encountered depending on the
age, sport, and the circumstances of the athlete's life—for example,
the person's own expectations, poor performance, not enough time

to practice, negativity of the coach, not enough playing time, pressure from parents, problems with teammates, frequent injuries, fatigue, not improving, nervousness about competition, conflict with others about participation, and too great a time commitment.

A third critical question that I ask during the assessment is, "What does it cost you to participate in your sport?" I mean this question in the broadest sense, not just financial. Obviously, when cost is high and fun and other benefits low, the athlete is unhappy and is likely to drop out or attempt to make adjustments aimed at improvement. Going into counseling with a professional who is experienced in sport psychology can be a valuable resource for helping the recreational athlete to maximize the benefits of sport participation and minimize the problems.

In this chapter, we look at some of the needs and circumstances that bring recreational athletes to seek a sport psychologist. Sometimes their performances and struggles are their reasons for seeking help. In other cases, their sport participation brought other life problems to the fore.

YOUTH SPORTS

Tim, a handsome, bright, verbal ten-year-old, was already an experienced athlete and an avid sports fan when we met. At age five, he had begun playing soccer and has since added swimming, basketball, baseball, and golf to his sports repertoire. As much as he loved playing sports, his participation had been seriously marred by severe anxiety before games and extreme hurt, disappointment, and damaged self-esteem whenever he played poorly or made a mistake. When his coach yelled or criticized him during a game or practice, his stomach would get upset, his muscles would tighten, and his mind would become confused. If his team lost when they were "supposed to win," he would withdraw and sulk for the better part of a day.

As an only child of two professional parents, Tim was accustomed to receiving encouragement, infrequent criticism, and lots of love and attention. In this home environment, he developed as a responsible, caring child who enjoyed setting and achieving high goals at an early age. Both of his parents described him as a "good kid." In school Tim earned all A's; he was popular with his peers and liked by his teachers.

Tim was referred to me by his parents who described him as taking his sports "too seriously" and not having enough fun. They had become increasingly concerned about his anguish and a few hints that this attitude was beginning to manifest in school and other areas of his life. There was no difficulty in getting Tim to agree to counseling; he thought it was "really cool" to have his own sport psychologist.

Tim is typical of many young recreational athletes with whom I've worked in recent years. Certainly sports can provide an excellent opportunity for young people to have fun, develop physical fitness, and learn life skills, but there is no guarantee that these experiences will occur. Today's youth sports are complex and present young participants with both positive opportunities and potential conflicts in their own values and expectations, as well as those of their parents and coaches.

Historic Changes in Youth Sports

With exceedingly rapid growth in the past twenty years, after-school, organized sports programs are estimated to attract approximately 50 percent of all children between the ages of eight and eighteen. This is in addition to those participating in scholastic sports.

The "good old days" of sandlot, child-organized, neighborhood-based sports have disappeared, replaced by highly structured, adult-supervised athletic activities. As a child, when I played baseball in the vacant lot across the street, there were no uniforms, no schedules, no regular teams, no time limits, no age or ability categories, no gender or size rules, no officials, no adult spectators, no photographs, no videotapes, no individual performance statistics, no win-loss records, no trophies, and no postseason banquet. Mom and Dad voiced no particular preference for our sports participation versus other neighborhood activities, as long as we stayed out of trouble, stayed within two blocks of home, and came in on time.

Unlike Tim's experience, there was very little pressure for us to perform. Each sandlot baseball game was a unique existential phenomenon, organized as we went along, leaving no material artifacts or written records. Except for a few residual memories, the teams and events of the day evaporated at sunset, to be totally reinvented and reconfigured on the next occasion.

Many of us did have fun. Our play was child directed and reflected child values. There were no commitments, and anyone who did not have fun quit by walking away or not playing at all. Although we learned a great deal about peer interaction, decision making, and conflict resolution, this type of sports participation provided only limited opportunities for learning sports skills, accepting discipline, setting and progressing toward long-term goals, self-discipline, self-control, working with a team, and developing self-esteem.

In contrast, today's child who participates in an after-school sport, like Tim, has probably been driven there by a parent who has made a carefully deliberated choice, paid an enrollment fee, purchased equipment, and has specific expectations. The activity is adult organized and supervised, and thus reflects adults' values. Although "Have fun!" may be the spoken admonition of parents and coaches, the structure and regimentation of the youth sports scene often convey an entirely different message, sometimes spoken, sometimes not: "WIN!"

Children and performances that contribute to winning are positively valued; those that do not are negatively valued. Thus, many young recreational athletes, like Tim, receive conflicting messages and don't know how to respond. Feeling tremendous pressure to perform well, they become anxious before games and feel terrible when they have performed poorly or made mistakes. Yes, they do have fun, but *only* when they and their team are doing well.

One attempt to reemphasize fun and learning in youth sports was introduced by Stewart Brand in the 1970s under the name of

"New Games" with the motto, "Play hard, play fair, nobody hurt." For example, in "infinity volleyball" the object is for all participants to cooperate with one another in keeping the ball going for as long as possible. In some communities, parents have organized youth sports leagues with modified rules, ones that encourage fun and discourage competition—for example, softball in which the child keeps batting until he gets a hit.

Such progressive movements have not attracted widespread participation, especially for children over age ten, for several reasons. Both children and their parents clearly prefer mainstream sports with their long histories and traditions. History and tradition connect the child's experiences with those of her parents and the culture. They also provide opportunities, for better or worse, to identify with sports figures who play the same sport they do.

Equally significant is the powerful influence of the media. Young people are products of a television culture and know sports through television, where sports teams and personalities are introduced to children in an interesting and exciting way. Encouraged and reinforced by their parents and peers, children often develop strong and loyal allegiances to particular teams and star players. Unfortunately, the values espoused by the media and culture of professional sports are clearly to win, with little attention paid to sportsmanship, quality of effort, and respect for opponents.

Through identification with professional athletes, at least as portrayed by the media, young athletes, like Tim, may internalize these values and bring them to their own playing field. This causes them to take the game "too seriously" and hold themselves, their teammates, and even coaches to inappropriately high standards of performance.

Counseling Young Athletes

In the past few years the number of young recreational athletes referred to me has increased substantially. Although the need for counseling with this group has probably been there for a long time, only recently have I noticed a positive shift toward awareness and acceptability of sport psychology services for children. Not long ago, the few young athletes whom I worked with came with considerable reluctance. They would slink into my waiting room with broad-brimmed hats and dark glasses, so as not to be recognized in a "shrink's" office. By contrast, when parents call today to make an appointment for their son or daughter and I ask how the child feels about working with me, I often hear, "It was her idea. She came home from practice one day and said, 'Dad, get me a sport psychologist.'" The field of sport psychology, as well as my own practice, has clearly benefited from favorable media coverage, especially during the Olympics, and from the openness with which many elite athletes now speak of their work with sport psychologists.

Although most of the young athletes I've worked with in the past have been adolescents, there has been an increase in referrals of preadolescents. My youngest client has been an eight-year-old figure skater who had severe anxiety before competition. Generally, the younger the athlete is, the more our emphasis should be on helping the child to be a good recreational athlete who has fun and maintains a healthy life balance. By adolescence, most of the athletes who come for services tend to be committed to sport and highly focused on improving performance, as well as having fun and maintaining life balance. With age, their concerns have progressed from simply having fun to developing skills and acquiring personal identity. The amount of pressure from others and from self has increased, as have the demands that they feel from other areas of life.

Unless there is serious personal or family dysfunction, my preference in working with the youngest recreational athletes is to emphasize fun and learning life skills through their sport. To be consistent with that, I attempt to complete interventions quickly and then taper off or go on an as-needed basis. Since many youngsters already have overcrowded schedules, I don't want to add another serious activity to their lives unless it is absolutely necessary. By providing a short, intensive, positive, and successful experience at this early age, I believe that the youngster will perceive me and my colleagues as desirable and effective resources they will feel comfortable calling on in the future when needed.

As in more traditional counseling and therapy, the younger the client is, the more involvement I have with the parents. Usually this is easily arranged since those under the age of sixteen don't drive and are brought to sessions by a parent who is available for this type of contact. Typically I have already spoken with one of the parents on the telephone and have the benefit of his or her observations and concerns. Most often I begin the first session by meeting with the child to establish rapport and begin the assessment process. During the final ten or fifteen minutes of the session, I invite the accompanying parent to join us as I briefly summarize my impressions and a plan of intervention. I am especially interested in observing the parent-child interactions, body language, and any other information that will help me assess the nature of their relationship.

Using both interview and the OSSI as tools, I address the question of why this youngster is participating in sport, from the perspectives of the child and each of the parents. One of my most important therapeutic goals is to raise consciousness and stimulate family discussions around this topic, in my office at first and later at home. Presenting parents and children with a list of fifteen commonly given reasons for sport participation helps them to evaluate the sport experience in terms other than just performing well and winning. Instead of asking the child after a baseball game, "Did your team win? How many hits did you have?" my goal is for parents to begin focusing on questions such as, "What happened that was fun? What did you learn?" I began doing this in response to my young clients' telling me how upset they would get at their parent for asking only performance questions.

The stereotypic parents who push their children in sports with too much emphasis on achievement, high-level performance, and winning do exist, and I see a fair share of them. In fact, such parents are highly likely to seek out sport psychologists as another resource in developing the talents of their young "superstars." Such

situations often involve personal and familial dysfunction and cannot be ignored. In such instances, I generally conduct some sessions
with one or both parents in which we discuss their roles and, I hope,
modify them. This is a sensitive and delicate area, since a direct,
confrontational approach is likely to lead to defensiveness and even
termination of the child's work with you.

For example, Ann, a very talented twelve-year-old gymnast, was
brought to me by her mother for help in overcoming her precompetition anxieties. The mother, who had Olympic dreams for her
daughter, attended all of her daughter's practices and competitions,
even scouting her opponents in advance. Although highly verbal
and animated when I met with her one-on-one, Ann behaved very
immaturely or withdrew whenever her mother attended a session
with us. Later, when I met individually with the mother to suggest
that her intensive involvement might be a source of pressure on
Ann, she became quite defensive. A short time later, I received a
message from the mother that Ann was "temporarily" discontinu-
ing her sessions with me due to an overcrowded time schedule. That
was the last I heard from her.

On the other hand, I have also worked with many parents, such
as Tim's, who genuinely have their children's best interest at heart
and need guidance in learning how to demonstrate interest and support for their child's sport participation, without being too demanding or overly involved. They are often frustrated to see the degree
to which their child has been influenced by values that they themselves oppose, such as overemphasis on winning and the ignoring
of sportsmanship and fun.

Working with young recreational athletes usually entails a combination of counseling and performance-enhancement techniques.
Often these young athletes have had no prior experience with sport
psychology techniques and respond quickly to training in the skills
of relaxation, attention focusing, and positive self-talk. In addition
to helping young athletes enjoy and benefit from their sport participation, I attempt to create a bridge that enables them to understand

how the lessons they learn in sports relate to everyday life. A large part of the counseling process consists of cognitive restructuring in which I attempt to refute irrational beliefs that young athletes often hold. Below are examples of typical issues that I address in my work with young athletes, along with the type of thinking that I am attempting to encourage.

- *Being a "developmental athlete."*   "Your uniform may look like a small-size version of a major league uniform, but the game is not the same. You play for a different reason than a professional player does. You are not a finished product. You are growing and changing in many ways, not just in sports. At every stage of development, there are things that are important. Having fun and doing your best is what's important now. Later, other things will become important."

- *Perfection.*   "The game is not perfect, the officials are not perfect, the coach is not perfect, and your parents are not perfect. So what makes you think you should be perfect? Babe Ruth hit 714 home runs. Do you know how many times he struck out? Would you believe 1,330? Think about that. How do you suppose he dealt with striking out each time?"

- *Anger.*   "Anger is a reaction to not getting your own way. In sports, there are many times that we don't get our own way. Sports and life are both complicated. In both, there are lots of people who are not getting their own way at any moment. Does anger make you a better batter? Does anger teach you how to perform better? If it did, you would probably try to think of more ways of making yourself angry. Anger results from the way in which you think about things. Let's look at some alternative ways of thinking about things."

- *Communication.*   "You need to help other people, especially your parents, understand you. By now you've probably figured out that even your mom can't really read your mind. Parents often don't know how to give you support. You have to teach them what helps you. What should they say or do when you're nervous before a big game? What should they say or do when you've had a poor performance and feel bad? Does the coach know that you're about to quit because you don't get enough playing time? Have you told your parents that you have trouble falling asleep because you're worried about not letting the team down?"

- *Unfairness.* "We all want to be treated fairly, but unfortunately, there is a lot of unfairness in both life and sport. Part of becoming a better person and a better athlete is learning how to accept unfairness. Do everything that you can to prevent or correct unfairness. Then let it go. If you don't, it eats away at you and makes you unhappy and interferes with paying attention to what you're doing."

- *Expectations.* "The more expectations we have of ourselves and others, the more we are likely to be disappointed. Expect yourself to do your best, but don't expect that you'll win because you're 'supposed' to beat this team that is 'no good.' Sports are based on the unexpected. Certainty wouldn't be much fun. If outcomes were predictable, we wouldn't have sports events. We'd just collect application forms and mail out the trophies."

- *Focus on what you can control.* "You usually can't choose your opponents or how good they are, so you really can't control winning. Don't focus your attention on anything that you can't control. If you do, it's a distraction and reduces the quality of your performance. Focus on what you can control: your thoughts, your focus, and your movements."

- *Accepting criticism.* "We can improve only when we know what we're doing right and what we're doing wrong. We can benefit from the criticism of coaches, teammates, and parents, especially when the criticism is offered in a kind way. When it's given in a kind way, we need to learn from it and not be too sensitive. That's not too hard to do if we've already accepted that we're not perfect. Sometimes when people are emotional, they are unkind in their criticism, and it hurts. In many cases, it helps to speak with them afterward and let them know how we feel. Some people will be more careful in the future, but not all people will. That's part of the unfairness that we have to learn to accept."

• *Role models.* "Who are the athletes you admire? What aspects about them do you admire? How do they handle poor performance? Anger? Disappointment? Do you know what they were doing when they were your age? What kind of people are they when they're not playing their sport? What bad times did they have to overcome?"

• *Your value as a person.* "Are you a better person when you hit a home run than when you strike out? Could you still be a worthwhile person even if you didn't play sports? How do other things help you to feel like a valuable or worthwhile person: your honesty, trying to do your best, being helpful and considerate of others, being a good friend, being generous, making people laugh?"

Let's look at how I applied these concepts to Tim.

Tim attended six sessions of counseling, initially once a week and then every two weeks, and now we meet on an as-needed basis. I met separately with his mother on one occasion and with both of his parents on another. Consistent with my initial impression, Tim turned out to be a psychologically healthy child living in a very nurturing home environment. He looked forward to our sessions and was easily able to recall specific game situations that were upsetting to him. With my encouragement, he maintained a simple journal in which he jotted notes when critical events, positive or negative, occurred.

It became clear that Tim had highly perfectionistic expectations of himself and others, leading to his frequent disappointment and anger. Although his parents had verbally told him that having fun, independent of achievement, was important, their own behavior contradicted their words. At times, both of his parents were highly achievement oriented and verbalized self-criticism whenever they fell short of their own goals or made mistakes. When I pointed this out to them, they agreed to loosen up and attempt to set a more appropriate example for their son. They also knew that this was something they needed to do for themselves as well.

At one point or another, Tim and I covered most of the items on the above agenda, and he seemed to be quite open and receptive to thinking about things differently. His parents were aware of my emphasis and supportive of this point of view. I took Tim through a brief course in relaxation training and guided him through several mental rehearsals in which he confronted typical stressful situations that he responded to in a new and effective manner. These sessions were tape-recorded for Tim to practice at home, sometimes with his parents listening as well.

Tim is now playing softball twice a week and planning to attend two sports camps this summer. According to Tim, as well as his parents, his enjoyment of sports has increased considerably. His upsets have been greatly reduced, although an occasional relapse will lead to a brief telephone refresher with me. He contacted me, for example, a few days ago. During a baseball game the day before, he had struck out each time at bat, unusual for Tim. While he managed it all right the first two times, after the third strikeout he began to cry and mentally "beat up on himself." It was his idea to call me. We talked for about fifteen minutes about Babe Ruth's 1,330 strikeouts and some of the other concepts that we'd discussed in our sessions. Tim felt better and had no need for an office visit. A week later, he left me a message that he was doing fine.

As Tim was walking out of my office after our final session, he stopped in midstep, turned around, and said, "Oh, by the way, I forgot to tell you. I've decided what I want to be when I grow up." "And what's that, Tim?" With a broad grin, he responded, "A sport psychologist."

WOMEN ATHLETES

Like many other women of her age, Laura, at forty-three, had discovered the pleasure of exercise and sport for the first time in her life. A year ago she began jogging with a woman friend in order to lose weight. It worked. Within a few weeks, she had lost five pounds and had made the pleasant discovery that jogging made her feel good about herself and enabled her to manage life stresses more effectively. She slept better, felt more energetic, and experienced a general feeling of well-being.

Shortly after, her friend changed jobs and was no longer available to jog with her. Laura quickly adjusted to jogging alone and discovered that she enjoyed this time by herself and the opportunity to think about anything she wanted to, without interruption. She increased her exercise from three or four times a week to jogging every day. She felt even better.

While shopping at the supermarket one day, after she had been jogging for several months, Laura picked up a flyer for a three-mile road race. With some trepidation, she decided to enter the race, "just to finish." Her daily jog now became a "run," and she trained with new sense of purpose.

As the day of the race approached, Laura's excitement and nervousness increased. When she talked about the upcoming race with Joe, her husband of twenty years, she was disappointed by his lack of interest and enthusiasm. Although he had encouraged her to start jogging and liked her slimmer figure, he couldn't understand why she "had" to run in a race. Her two children, Kathleen, age sixteen, and Scott, age thirteen, were preoccupied with their own interests and as usual didn't care as long as it didn't affect them.

The Sunday morning of the race, Laura rose an hour earlier than usual and left the house while the rest of the family slept. How nice it would have been if someone had written, "Good Luck, Mom!" on the kitchen chalkboard, instead of, "Don't forget to pick up my stuff at the dry cleaners."

The race turned out to be more difficult than Laura had ever imagined. Carried away by her own excitement and energized by the other runners, she had run the first mile much faster than she had ever run before and was out of breath and aching all over. After she slowed her pace, she felt better but still hurt. The pain and discomfort were quickly forgotten, however, when she crossed the finish line and was loudly cheered by other runners and spectators: "Good job...looking great...way to go...you did it!" Never in her entire life could Laura remember having been cheered, and now, at age forty-three, she had finished a race and was being cheered by a group of total strangers! This was moment to be shared, and it was shared, but not with those closest to her.

Over the next year, Laura continued her daily runs, gradually increasing her speed, distance, and the amount of time she spent running. Although her finishing times never became important to her, she raced one or two times a month. Shortly after her first race, she met and befriended several other runners, who invited her to join their running club, where she became an active member and recently accepted the position as editor of the club's newsletter.

During this year Laura felt better and better about herself. She enjoyed her new friends and activities and felt liked and respected by the running community. She enjoyed the changes in her own body as she became fit, strong, and fast. At home, however, things were not going well. Joe's attitude toward Laura's running went from indifferent to negative to hostile. He became jealous of her new friends, especially male runners, and often mocked them. Both he and the children resented the time that she spent away from the family, even though she completed most of her homemaker tasks in an efficient manner. Although she always invited Joe to come to her races and club activities, he rejected all such invitations, saying he wasn't going to be a "cheerleader" for anyone. Overweight and spending much time in front of the television set, Joe became angrier and angrier at his wife and wished that she could just go back and be like she was before, when "they were both happy."

Laura began counseling with me after an unusually bitter and nasty argument with Joe. She had tried to discuss her tentative plans with him to attend a one-week runners' camp with a few of her friends from the club. When she didn't yield to his immediate disapproval, he became increasingly angry and "went ballistic," accusing her of not loving him, not caring about their children, becoming selfish, thinking she was too good for her family, and having an affair with one of her running friends. Laura felt deeply hurt, confused, angry, and guilty. Why, she asked, had doing something that was so good for her had such a negative impact on her husband and children? She felt alone and misunderstood. Why could Joe go fishing in Canada for a week each year with his buddies, but she couldn't go to a running camp twenty miles away?

At all ages and levels, women's participation in sports has dramatically increased in the past twenty-five years, and with it has come considerable conflict. During this time, we have seen significant changes in the role of women in our society, as demands for fairness and equality of opportunity have led to the increased participation of women in the workplace, in professions and job roles previously monopolized by men, and in the restructuring of the family and men's roles.

One important landmark in the changing role of women in sports was the passage of the 1972 Title IX of the Education Amendments Act, which requires schools and universities to provide for the equal development and support of sports programs for men and women. Although full compliance has not been attained, the impact of this legislation has been profound. For example, in 1972, approximately 31,000 women participated in intercollegiate sports programs; in 1995, the number had reached 120,000. At the high school level, the figures were approximately 300,000 in 1971; they are 2.4 million today.

Social change is never easy and is often accompanied by ambiguity, opposition, controversy, and conflict. The old ways are gone, but there is no clear consensus on the new. The conflict is especially turbulent for those in the transitional generation, like Laura and Joe, reared with one set of values and now having to function in a world with a different set. Because of rapid societal changes, it is difficult understanding the woman athlete without considering her age and generation.

The Elderly

Laura's mother, Louise, now sixty-eight, was born in 1929 and grew up in a time when very few girls and women participated in sports. Her own lifelong athletic participation consisted of mandatory physical education classes, which she detested. Her high school sponsored intramural sports for girls but no interscholastic teams. Girls who participated in sports were considered to be "masculine," the brunt of unkind jokes, and not particularly popular with either boys or girls. Although Louise did not attend college, in those days 90 percent of all college students were male and almost all of intercollegiate sports were male, at least those that received newspaper and radio coverage. Women's colleges, which did have both intramural and some intercollegiate sports events, received next to no publicity.

Sports in general played a much smaller role in the American lifestyle than today, and even the Olympic Games attracted much less interest and attention than now. Although there were well-known women athletes during Louise's formative years, for most of her generation, these women were at best interesting, but not accepted as role models.

During her middle years, Louise was a conscientious homemaker, focusing much of her time and energy on the needs of her husband and three children. Child rearing, shopping, cooking, laundry, housekeeping, and managing the family social events took up most of her time, and there was no such thing as "leisure" activities. The women in her neighborhood, who met for coffee and talk a few times a week, all led lives very much like hers. If any of them had participated in sports as a youngster, she had given it up after high school and had no reason to talk about it. None of her friends talked about sports or participated in exercise or sports. She was aware that wealthier women, who had leisure time, belonged to clubs and played tennis and golf—sports acceptable for women.

When Billy, her first son, showed interest in playing Little League baseball, she and her husband were enthusiastic and soon became ardent fans. The day the whole family went to the sporting goods store to get

Billy outfitted was an event that they talked about for years. Louise attended all of Billy's games, learned about baseball, and organized the annual bake sale that raised funds for his team.

A few years later, when Laura expressed an interest in trying out for the newly organized girl's high school basketball team, Louise had serious doubts. Weren't girls too fragile for such strenuous physical activity? Couldn't she hurt herself and jeopardize her ability to bear children? How would others see her daughter? Would boys make fun of her and see her as a tomboy? Would they stop asking her for dates? Was it proper for her to expose so much of her body publicly? People might get the wrong idea. Today, in therapy, Laura doesn't recall any of the details, except that her parents opposed her playing basketball, and she never went to the tryouts.

Widowed five years ago, Louise lives by herself in a retirement apartment complex. Still in good health, she is active and enjoys being with her friends and participating in the structured social activities at the senior center. At the age of sixty-six, she enrolled in a low-impact aerobics class and goes for a brisk walk with two of her neighbors each morning.

She is very proud of Laura's running and plans to attend one of her races the next time she visits. Her refrigerator is covered with photos and newspaper clippings of her favorite basketball star, her granddaughter, Kathleen, who is a starter on her high school team. Although her knowledge is limited, Louise has become an ardent fan of the Chicago Bulls and watches many of their games on television. She enjoyed watching the U.S. Olympic women's basketball game and looks forward to the first season of the Women's National Basketball Association.

At times, she wishes she had been born later.

Although the role of sports in our culture, and especially women's sports, changed drastically during Louise's lifetime, the impact on her was minimal. She lived most of her active years following the values that she had learned as a child. By the time major changes in the roles of women in society and life had become widespread, her child-rearing years were over. Now, as a senior citizen, with diminished responsibilities, considerable leisure time, and simpler interpersonal relationships, she finds herself comfortable and accepting of many of the changes. She likes the spirit of the young women who supervise the recreation program at the center, and becoming an exerciser was easier for her because she began in a group of women her own age.

As a counselor, you may see women of this generation in your practice. Some, like Louise, are already benefiting from regular exercise. Others may be encouraged to exercise as a means of coping more effectively with depression, anxiety, and self-esteem issues. Some will need help in dealing with their adult children who may express resentments about their upbringing. Others may feel guilt and resentment resulting from the values that guided their lives, which they now view negatively and wish they had changed earlier.

The Young

Kathleen, now sixteen, was born nine years after Title IX became law. She was three years old when the International Olympic Committee reluctantly sanctioned its first Women's Marathon in Los Angeles in 1984. By the time she started kindergarten, high school and colleges throughout the country had established and significantly expanded women's sports. She grew up in a world in which she saw elite women athletes compete in the Olympic Games, marathons, professional golf, and other sports. She saw role models that she could identify with— women who could train hard, work hard, compete hard, sweat, and still preserve their femininity.

When Kathleen began playing sports, she enjoyed developing her physical strengths and putting them to a test. Unlike her grandmother, the thought never occurred to her that she might be too fragile to participate or that strenuous activity could threaten her future child-bearing capability. Both of her parents enthusiastically supported her trying out for the basketball team, and her father volunteered to give her pointers on shooting a free throw. Both parents were hopeful that she might play well enough to earn a college scholarship, which would help to reduce their financial burden.

Although considerably less conflicted than either her mother or grandmother about the role of women in sports, Kathleen was not without her worries. At times, basketball seemed to take up too much of her time. She didn't have a regular boyfriend and wondered if it had anything to do with her being an athlete. At times, the coach was pushing her to be more competitive and aggressive, something that was difficult for her to do. While she strived to improve her skills, it bothered her when other girls on the team became jealous of her starting position or the number of points she scored in a game. Several times when she should have shot the ball, she passed to a teammate in hope that this would increase her popularity.

Like Kathleen, many young women of her generation have issues associated with their sports participation that may bring them to a counselor or sport psychologist. In spite of social progress, there remains the issue of achieving athletic excellence and preserving femininity, however that may be defined by the individual and the cultural environment. As higher levels of athletic competition are reached, the personal characteristics required for success—assertive behavior, competence, strength, achievement orientation, self-focused attitude, independence, tough-mindedness, and competitive drive to beat others—have traditionally been encouraged in males and discouraged in females. In any individual woman athlete, striving for excellence, feeling good about oneself, and receiving the acceptance of others may be jeopardized by the conflicts that our culture places on her. The sport psychologist with an understanding and appreciation of these issues can help women athletes in the process of finding their balance.

The Middle Generation

Laura, who started running at age forty-two, represents the transitional generation of women athletes—those who were reared before the major social changes and Title IX and who raised their children after these changes. Laura experienced little or no conflict about her daughter's participation in sports. She applauded the social changes that enabled Kathleen to play girls' basketball and other sports with the open approval of other parents, neighbors, and the community. She was even pleasantly surprised at her own mother's support of Kathleen's athletic endeavors, something she had longed for during her own childhood.

Conflict didn't arise until she began her own athletic participation as a recreational runner. Then, rather suddenly, as she gradually became accustomed to her new good feelings and improved self-image, she found herself in serious conflict with the role demands of her husband and her children.

Laura's issues are fairly typical of a woman who becomes an athlete at midlife. Like her daughter, she struggles with the internal conflict between sport participation and maintaining her own feelings of femininity. Since her performance and competitive goals are modest, she is spared having to deal with many of the conflicts that Kathleen must face. Nevertheless, a woman in her middle years who goes through such changes in self-perception and reclaims part of her life often runs into conflict with others in her family system. The more compliant, nurturing, and other-centered she had been in the past, the greater the opposition she will experience. Also, the more compliant, nurturing, and other-centered she had been, the more she is likely to resent the opposition of what she sees as reasonable accommodation from her family members. After all, she's done so much for them; why can't they be supportive of her now? The answer is that they have been "spoiled."

Many women, of course, do live in psychologically healthy families where their positive changes are supported and reinforced. I've never run a marathon without seeing at least ten handmade signs along the course reading something like, "GO MOM!" held by a proud "cheerleader" husband while a child or two waited at his side eager to spot mom and hand her orange slices.

After three months, Laura continues therapy on a weekly basis. Although she runs each day and races occasionally, she rarely talks with her family about this important aspect of her life. It helps "keep the peace," she says. She feels increasingly alienated from her family and spends increasing time with her running friends, with whom she feels accepted, valued, and emotionally supported. She has developed a special friendship with Peter, an experienced marathon runner who has shown her interest. Recently divorced, he is empathetic to Laura, having experienced a similar situation in his own marriage. She appreciates the attention that he shows her and has become increasingly comfortable with him. Recently he has made several physical overtures toward her, which both excite and scare her. She finds him very attractive and has begun to have fantasies about having a relationship with him. She reminds herself that she's a moral person, still married to Joe, and vows to resist acting on her fantasies.

Psychological testing at the time of her first session revealed a fairly healthy, well-adjusted person, well above average in intelligence and high in creativity. As a full-time homemaker for most of her marriage, Laura had few challenges that put her abilities to a rigorous test. The profile also indicated relatively low scores on assertiveness.

We discussed the concept of assertiveness in our sessions and why each person's needs are important and not to be ignored. At my suggestion, she read several books on assertiveness and began practicing new ways of communicating with others. Although her increased assertive behaviors made her feel better about herself, they increased the tension at home.

After some time, I suggested that it might be beneficial to invite Joe to participate in several joint counseling sessions. As she predicted, Joe refused, saying that he was not the one who needed help. This refusal added to the hurt and anger that had been building for a long time.

Laura is seriously contemplating separation and divorce. If it weren't for the children, she'd move out now, at least on a trial basis. While increasingly attracted to Peter, she vows not to be sexual with him, but at times she wonders if she has the strength to resist her strong feelings for him, spurred by the lack of caring and affection from Joe.

Joe continues to think that everything was all right in his marriage until his wife began running and then changed. Laura knows that her discovery of running and rediscovery of neglected aspects of her self merely brought to the surface the dysfunction that had existed in her marriage for a long time. She knows that it will not continue.

THE INJURED ATHLETE

At sixteen, Stacey had been a gymnast for more than half of her life. Now, in her senior year in high school, she had high expectations for making the national finals in two months. In recent weeks, she had become worried about occasional sharp lower back pains that occurred during her landings. Fearing that she might be restricted from participating, she withheld this information from her parents, teammates, and coach. Finally, when the pain became severe, she told her mother, and together they went to her doctor. The doctor diagnosed a stress fracture in two of her vertebrae, and Stacey was placed in a back brace, restricted from all athletic participation for at least three months.

An involuntary restriction, interruption, or end of one's athletic participation is a stressful experience. The recreational tennis player, skier, softball player, golfer, or bowler loses something of value when unable to enjoy the customary level of sport participation. To understand what they have lost and help them to cope with the loss, we need to understand what significance their sport plays in their life. I use a clinical interview and the OSSI, with its fifteen reasons for sport participation, to help me understand the role of sport in the client's life.

Fortunately, most sports injuries heal, and most athletes are able to return to their previous level of participation. In my practice, I work closely with fellow sports medicine professionals: physical therapists, trainers, physicians, orthopedic surgeons, podiatrists, and massotherapists who specialize in working with athletes. Often they refer clients to me who are having psychological difficulties in coping with their injury and its consequences. I also refer clients to them when an athlete I've been working with becomes injured and has not received appropriate medical attention. I emphasize the need for seeing medical professionals who specialize in sports medicine. They understand and are respectful of their clients' need to participate in sport and are motivated to help them return to full participation as soon as possible. Highly competent but not sport-minded medical professionals are more likely to recommend temporary or permanent abstention from the sport with such statements as, "Just don't run anymore, and you'll be fine."

The sport psychologist can help the injured athlete. By identifying the needs that were satisfied by sport participation, we can help the athlete discover temporary or permanent alternative activities. We can also help the athlete change from feeling like a helpless victim to becoming an active participant in his treatment and recovery. We know that recovery occurs more quickly with less psychological distress when the athlete experiences the following:

- A clear understanding of the injury, treatment options, likely timetable for recovery, and instructions for prevention of a similar injury in the future

- Participation in treatment decisions

- Time-oriented, frequent, measurable goals that accurately indicate progress toward complete rehabilitation

- Specific, concrete, daily exercises or treatments that the athlete can perform in order to achieve the goals

- Frequent contact with a social support system, especially with athletes with whom he usually participates

- Accepting an alternate role in his sport community until he is able to return (e.g., a runner who helps organize a race that he usually runs)

- Positive affirmations and positive self-talk

- Mental imagery related to healing

Additionally, try to help the injured athlete use the time normally consumed by his sport for beneficial, goal-oriented activity. For example, I often point out how this is a good opportunity to spend more time learning, practicing, and perfecting the mental skills necessary for his sport.

If the injury is permanent and the athlete is unable to return to his sport, this situation may precipitate a personal crisis that will require intensive counseling. At times the client may experience denial; at other times he may be flooded by powerful emotions such as depression, anger, and resentment. Support and stabilization are the initial priorities that need to be addressed before the client is ready to look at the long-range goal of finding appropriate replacement activities. Some have suggested that athletes dealing with involuntary termination from their sport go through the same stages of coping that Elizabeth Kübler-Ross has identified in terminally ill patients: denial, anger, bargaining, depression, and acceptance.

THE AGING ATHLETE

In spite of practicing longer and harder, Steve, a sixty-seven-year-old veteran golfer, has watched his handicap increase by a point or two during each of the past few years. Although not pleased, he refocuses his attention on how much he enjoys the outdoors, being with lifelong friends, and the benefits of this exercise.

After thirty-five years of recreational downhill skiing, Jim, at age sixty, finds himself becoming fearful of the more difficult runs and prefers those that are less challenging. Because of this, he loses self-respect and feels "less of a man." He wonders if he should stop skiing altogether.

With the advancement of age, there is a gradual loss of physical strength, speed, flexibility, coordination, and mental sharpness that results in lowered performance. An active, healthy lifestyle will slow the aging process. Appropriate decreases in frequency, duration, and intensity of sport activity can prolong the athlete's participation, but ultimately the decline is inevitable. The age at which this becomes noticeable and the rate of decline vary considerably with each person and the physical and mental demands of the sport.

In some respects, the issues of aging athletes are similar to those of injured athletes. Both experience an involuntary decline in their level of proficiency. In most cases, however, injured athletes recover and return to former levels of performance. Aging athletes will not. Their decline may be slowed down but not reversed. The psychological impact of these changes varies with the meaning and importance that sport participation has had for the individual. Those whose pleasure derived from competition and high levels of proficiency will notice the decline first and have the greatest difficulty in adjusting to these unwelcome changes. Less competitive athletes, who have enjoyed their participation for other reasons, will be more tolerant of the decline and have less difficulty adjusting. Ultimately, if we live long enough, the day will come when we are no longer able to meet even the minimal physical demands and must cease playing altogether.

Preparing recreational athletes for these inevitable changes and counseling them through the process is a valuable service that the sport psychologist can provide. As always, it is important for the athlete to know which of her needs are being satisfied through sport so that viable alternatives can be developed. The athlete who antic-ipates these changes and makes gradual adjustments will have an easier adjustment than those who give it little forethought. In many sports, these changes are eased with age-graded competition or "senior" events that provide a healthy outlet for those whose com-petitive instincts still run high.

As our ability to participate diminishes with age, new opportu-nities also arise. Those who are open and flexible can remain in their familiar sports environments, maintaining recognition and contact with sporting friends, if they are willing to accept new roles, such as teaching, coaching, officiating, organizing events, holding club officer positions, writing, editing a newsletter, and speaking about their experiences to a wide variety of audiences.

The group that now approaches its retirement years is the first generation of Americans who have enjoyed lifelong recreational sports in such great numbers. They will be the first generation in need of professionals who can help them make a successful transition to a less active lifestyle.

We have explored only a few of the ways in which sport psychologists can provide valuable services to recreational athletes. With large and growing numbers of diverse participants, covering almost the entire life span, the possibilities for developing meaningful services to this population are immense.

Next, we'll move up the continuum of commitment to consider the psychological needs of the highly committed and elite athlete.

7

Working with Committed
and Elite Athletes

Committed athletes live for their sport. Goal oriented and devoted to the work ethic, they may have already achieved at a high level and have even higher aspirations for the future. They devote considerable time and money in order to participate in their sport and to develop their abilities. They are willing to make major sacrifices in other areas of life in order to participate successfully in their sport. Although they love their sport, their love is conditional and requires at least satisfactory levels of performance in order to be enjoyed. Committed athletes cover a wide range of individuals and sports, from twelve-year-old figure skaters, to serious amateur golfers, to high school football players striving for Big Ten scholarships, to middle-aged marathoners, Olympic hopefuls, Olympians, and professional athletes.

Although many, and probably most, committed athletes do perform at high levels, being a committed athlete is an attitude toward one's sport and does not necessarily correspond with proficiency, as judged by objective standards or by other people. Some committed athletes are focused on meeting their own internal definitions of high-level performance, which they may adjust for age and experience. For others, this is insufficient; they strive persistently to win games and championships, as well as set records.

The elite athlete is a committed athlete who has succeeded. Natural talent, diligence, and commitment to sport have led to high levels of achievement and recognition. Generally the term *elite* is reserved for those few who have competed successfully at the highest levels of national and international competition in their sport.

The issues addressed in the previous chapter on recreational athletes are equally relevant to committed and elite athletes. Some committed and elite athletes are still in their youth, many are women, and all deal with concerns of injury and the aging process. Like their recreational counterparts, committed athletes struggle to maintain balance in life, between sport and other priorities, although their definition of balance is different from that of recreational athletes.

These athletes may come to you for performance-enhancement services, counseling, or both. Their life problems run the full range that you've already experienced in working with your clinical clients: anxiety, depression, self-esteem, relationships, stress, plus other presenting problems that may be more frequent in some athlete populations, such as perfectionism, eating disorders, and substance abuse.

In order to provide clinical consultation or performance-enhancement services to committed and elite athletes, it is essential that you have appropriate sport-specific knowledge and skills. Since most of these athletes already have well-developed mental skills, it will require special expertise to identify specific gaps in their mental skills and develop an effective training program. You'll also want to be careful not to interfere with ongoing habits that have been successful for the athlete, even if they seem unconventional to you.

Essential to the process is establishing trust and credibility with the committed athlete, especially if you don't participate in the client's sport or even know much about it.

GAINING SPORT-SPECIFIC KNOWLEDGE

In Chapter Two, we discussed ways of increasing your knowledge and skills in the techniques of sport psychology. Before beginning to work with athlete clients, you may be asking yourself such questions as: "Do I need to play golf in order to work with golfers?" or more generally, "How much do I need to know about a specific sport in order to be effective?" Let me begin to answer your questions with a true story.

> In fall 1996, Lauren Bass, a young equestrian with whom I had worked intensively, won the prestigious Maclay National Championship for junior equitation riders. In the final round at Madison Square Garden, with live ESPN television cameras focused on her, she was required by the rules to jump the course on another competitor's horse, one she had never ridden before. The newspaper account of her success included Lauren's description of her first few moments on the strange horse: "The horse was extremely sensitive and nervous. Usually when a horse is nervous, I get nervous too. But I tried to relax so the horse would relax, too. And the horse did." Later Lauren told me that her ability to relax in this stressful situation was a direct result of our work together.

Although I have enjoyed considerable success in working with equestrians and have developed a favorable reputation among serious competitive riders in my area, I have never participated in this sport. In fact, the last time I was even on a horse, JFK was president.

You may be an avid sports fan, with considerable knowledge of sports, or you may follow a few sports rather casually or even not at all. Your own sports participation may be vast and intense, or quite limited. Whatever the case, you need not be deterred from integrating sport psychology in your practice. The consensus among professional sport psychologists is that you don't need to be a participant in a specific sport in order to be effective in working with athletes from that sport, nor do you have to be an avid sports fan in order to practice sport psychology. Nevertheless, some degree of serious sport participation in your own life will be quite helpful. Most important, you do need to prepare yourself and do your homework as you begin to work with athletes from a sport with which you are not familiar.

There are two important considerations with regard to sport-specific issues: having sufficient knowledge and understanding of the sport and developing credibility among your clients even when you don't participate in their sport.

PREPARATION FOR WORKING WITH A "NEW" SPORT

My intensive experience with serious hunter-jumper equestrians began several years ago when I was approached by local competitive riders to conduct a mental skills workshop for their group. Aware of my sport-specific limitations with regard to equestrians, I accepted the invitation and immediately began to do my homework, as I always do when working with a new sport. Here are some of the tactics that I have found to be useful and effective in orienting myself to a new sport:

• *Be open about your limitations and your strengths.* Openly acknowledge that you haven't participated in the sport and that you don't know much about it, when that is the case. Indicate your willingness and desire to learn. Build your professional credibility on common ground. When asked if you participate in this sport yourself, respond with such statements as these: "Although I don't ride, I am a competitive runner, and I know what it feels like to work on long-range goals, to train hard, to be nervous just before a big event, and sometimes to be disappointed with my performance." "No, I'm not a rider, but I'm not here to teach you riding. You have experienced trainers or coaches who do that very well. I teach mental skills. I've done that with athletes from over twenty-five different sports. These skills are pretty much the same across all sports, although how they're used may be different."

• *Learn from the experts.* In preparing for my equestrian workshop, I contacted two of the top trainers in the area, who were very supportive of teaching mental skills to riders. They agreed to an interview, which I conducted at their barn, where I could begin to familiarize myself with the environment and culture in which equestrians train and compete. My questions were similar to those that I'd asked figure skating coaches and coaches from other sports. How much of successfully competing as an equestrian is mental? What are the mental skills that a successful equestrian uses? Can you describe and mentally replay one of your own best performances for me? What were you thinking and feeling at each stage? What aspects of the environment were you attending to? What distractions do you have to block out? What was your self-talk at each stage? When working with an individual athlete, the same types of questions will help you to understand the sport and its specific mental demands.

Interviewing experts not only yields useful information but also affords a chance for you to establish your credibility with local recognized authorities in the sport. This can be instrumental in getting future referrals as well as an approving head nod when your name comes up. Most local experts I've approached have been receptive and supportive of my efforts.

• *Television and videotapes.* If the sport that you're preparing to work with receives television coverage, this provides another excellent learning opportunity. I usually videotape the coverage so that I can view it at my convenience and fast-forward to critical learning situations. Good commentators, often those who themselves have participated in the sport, will discuss the mental demands and how the athlete deals with them. In sports that don't receive media coverage, commercially produced videotapes are often available.

When working with an individual athlete, ask if they have any videotapes of their own performances. I have a television set and videocassette recorder in my office so that my client and I can view the videotapes together. This is a quick way of getting a sense of the sport as well as learning about the client. Using stop action and slow motion, I ask the client to describe her thoughts, feelings, distractions, and so on at various stages of her performance. Such videotapes are commonly available for athletes who participate in figure skating, gymnastics, show jumping, and other individual sports.

•   *Books and magazines.*   Depending on the depth of knowledge that I'm attempting to acquire about a sport, I may purchase a book or two that describes the basic rules, fundamental skills, and strategies of a given sport. I also have in my reference library books of rules for most sports. If I'm fortunate, there may some good books available on the psychological skills for that particular sport, written by a reputable sport psychologist, rather than a motivational speaker.

There are specialty magazines for almost all sports. If I am preparing for a major involvement with a given sport, as I've done with figure skating and equestrian competition, I ask coaches or clients to recommend a good magazine, to which I then subscribe. Such magazines provide good insights into the general culture of the sport, and the content of articles is a good index of the concerns of the participants. This is also a good source of sport-specific anecdotes and stories that will be important for you to use when working with your athletes.

It's a good idea to familiarize yourself with the big names in the sport, since your clients will make reference to them. Sport-specific books and magazines also provide a quick method for learning the specialized vocabulary and slang. Knowing and using these terms appropriately is essential to your credibility. For example, equestrians ride in a "ring" and figure skaters skate in a "rink." Figure skaters are affiliated with a "skating club," equestrians with a "barn."

•   *Sport psychology colleagues and experts.*   Once you have become immersed in preparing to work with a given sport, you may benefit from interaction with colleagues or experts who have worked with athletes of that sport. I've contacted sport psychologists several times who are known for working with athletes from a given sport, either by letter or telephone. Most have readily shared materials and ideas with me. I make these contacts only after doing considerable preparation on my own. By this time, I usually have a few specific questions for them, or I ask for their thoughts on one or two particular ideas. Recently I've found the Sportpsy mail list on the Internet to be an excellent resource for this type of dialogue. (The Appendix lists Internet resources.)

Do you have to go through this comprehensive process each time you work with an athlete from a sport that is new to you? Not necessarily. What you've just read is my scenario for preparing for major involvement with a sport. Usually that means preparing for workshop presentations and cultivating a professional relationship with the coaches and other referral sources. You don't always need to go through this entire procedure for each individual athlete from a new sport.

I believe that you can be effective in helping an individual athlete by quickly understanding exactly what performance behaviors are expected of him and the circumstances in which the behaviors are to be performed. In working with Andy Eminger, a college football punter, I didn't need to develop a comprehensive understanding of the entire game and culture of college football in order to help him. Instead, Andy taught me just what I needed to know: the mental and physical attributes of a successful punt, the environment in which he punts, the aspects of the internal and external environment to which he should be paying attention, the internal and external distractions that have sometimes impaired his performance, and his optimal level of arousal for performing well. With this information, I was able to plan a successful individual mental skills training program for Andy that enabled him to manage his arousal more effectively and maintain his concentration under pressure.

STARTING TO WORK
WITH COMMITTED ATHLETES

By now you're probably getting anxious to get started. If you've been approached by an athlete whose needs are within your expanding range of competence, great! If not, you may have to reach out in order to expand your practice into this new arena. Although I go into this in more detail in Chapter Eight, here are a few tips.

Choosing a Sport

Maximize your strengths. Start with a sport that you understand well as a result of your own experience as a participant or coach. Review your understanding of the mental demands of that sport and techniques that can be taught to or sharpened for athletes in the sport. Use your contacts with athletes and coaches to indicate the availability of your services. Consider introducing yourself to that sport community by volunteering to give a presentation at a coaches' meeting or clinic, or conduct a small, low-cost workshop for athletes and coaches. This is a quick way of establishing professional visibility in your new area. Produce attractive flyers and handouts that will be retained and lead to referrals, both now and in the future. If you don't have a specific sports background that lends itself to this process, select a sport for your practice development, one that has a sufficient number of serious recreational participants in your area and which you already know something about.

If you're just beginning and lack an experience base, I suggest choosing a "closed-skill" rather than an "open-skill" sport. In a closed-skill sport—for example, diving, gymnastics, figure skating, target shooting, field and track, and golf—the athlete executes preplanned behaviors in a relatively controlled environment. In the performance situation, there are no other athletes in motion or a moving ball or any other object. There is nothing that the athlete has to react to, so the behavior unfolds under the control of the athlete. Since there are few uncontrolled environmental variables, working with these sports is usually simpler than open-skill sports. Athletes who participate in these sports generally perform solo, are judged by very high, perfectionistic standards, and feel a tremendous amount of personal responsibility for their performances. It is difficult for them to blame teammates, opponents, or other external factor for a substandard performance. Therefore, they are especially good candidates for mental skills training and often seek out the services of sport psychologists.

Working with Your First Committed Athlete

The big day has arrived. Your first committed athlete client is sitting in the waiting room, and in a few minutes you'll open the door and introduce yourself to him and take a big step in a new direction for your practice. You're a bit nervous. Remembering some of the sport psychology techniques that you've learned in the past few months, you take a deep, slow breath, hold it for a few seconds, and then slowly exhale. The edge is off your anxiety. Now you close your eyes for a few seconds, and imagine yourself inviting the client into your office, introducing yourself to him, establishing rapport, and conducting an assessment according to your mental outline. You open your eyes and think to yourself, "This is very similar to the thousands of clinical first sessions that I've conducted. The differences are small and I am prepared. Yes, I am prepared." Feeling excited and competent, you rise from your chair with a smile on your face and begin walking to the waiting room to greet your new client.

Several months ago you began preparing yourself for expanding your practice into sport psychology. After considerable reflection, you decided that a good starting point would be to develop your skills for working with serious recreational golfers. Although you played golf during high school and college, you gave up the sport while in graduate school and have not had the time to return to it. Nevertheless, you once played a respectable round and have a good understanding of the sport and its mental demands.

Since making your decision to work with golfers, you have immersed yourself in an intensive self-study program to prepare for this new venture. You read several books on sport psychology techniques and found them to be very similar to the cognitive-behavioral therapy that you've been practicing for years. Next, you read several books on the mental aspects of golf by respected sport psychologists and interviewed the club pro at a local country club. The past few Sundays you watched several golf tournaments on television and took notes. After putting it all together, you accepted the club pro's invitation to give a short, informal talk to twenty club members on the "Mental Aspects of Golf" at a recent luncheon. During the talk you demonstrated relaxation and imagery techniques.

Your new client enters your office and sits down in a comfortable chair. Chuck is a sixteen-year-old high school student and avid golfer. He was referred to you by his father, who was impressed by your presentation at the country club and thought Chuck might benefit from individual mental skills training. The young man is nervous at first, but you are able to put him at ease quickly. Chuck has been playing golf since he was nine. He appears to have a natural talent for the game and handicap of two. During the past two years, he was the number one player on his high school team and has done well in the many tournaments he plays each summer. There is no doubt that Chuck is a committed athlete.

Chuck is very clear about his need for help. He has three major concerns: (1) His best play occurs during everyday practice rounds. His scores are always worse during a tournament, even if it's on a familiar course. (2) He becomes very nervous before tournaments and has difficulty sleeping the night before and eating breakfast. He arrives at the course tense and with a nervous stomach. (3) He often becomes very angry at himself after missing an easy shot. Chuck knows that these problems are all "mental" and has come to you for help.

You tell Chuck that these types of problems are familiar to you and that you are optimistic about being able to help him. Before continuing, you explain that as a clinical professional you work with the "whole person" and that although your focus will be primarily on performance enhancement, you will want to know some other things about him as a person and how golf fits into his life. You assure him that he can feel free to bring up any concerns he might have, whether or not they are golf related. At this point you explain client confidentiality and professional boundaries and ask him about any concerns he has about these issues.

Intake Interview

During the remainder of the session, you interview Chuck as the first step in the process of assessing his needs and planning your intervention. You may have your own outline for a first interview or you may borrow from the one that I use. My initial interview with a sport psychology client is aimed at accomplishing five purposes:

1. *Establishing rapport.* The goal is to help the client to feel comfortable with me and talk about things that make him feel good and positive. What's going well? What do you like about your sport? I present myself to the client as someone who cares about him, is competent, and is comfortable to work with.

2. *Understanding the role of sport in his life.* What level of athlete is this on the continuum? What sacrifices do you make for your sport? What do you get back? Is this satisfactory? How would you like things to be a year from now? Who gives you emotional support? Who seems to pressure you?

3. *Screening for clinical problems.* Are there any possible serious psychological problems that I, as a clinician, need to be aware of? What are the sources of stress in your life? How severe are the stresses? How well are you dealing with them? How do they affect your performance? What are your habits (eating, sleeping, tobacco,

alcohol, drugs, medications)? Are your relationships helpful, stressful, or mixed?

4.   *Setting goals.*   The client and I agree on goals for our work together. For Chuck, these may be the presenting problems that he stated at the beginning of the session, or they may have been modified or added to. If any clinical issues were identified, these should be discussed and dealt with in an appropriate fashion. In some instances, they might be included in the goals, or it might be appropriate to refer the client to another clinician for these. This decision may be based on your particular clinical expertise, and whether it is effective to work intensively with performance and clinical issues within the same relationship. For example, Chuck may reveal that he feels unfair pressure from his father to succeed in golf. You may decide to address that problem in your work together. On the other hand, if Chuck has issues of sexual orientation, which you are not trained to work with, you might suggest a referral to another clinician for help in this area.

5.   *Closure.*   Where do we go from here? The session ends with my giving a brief explanation of how we will proceed. I usually suggest weekly sessions for five times, then a review and adjustment, if appropriate. Sessions are scheduled, fees and payment policies discussed, and homework assigned. Usually my client will take home the Mental Skills Assessment Form with instructions for completing the form and mailing it back to me as soon as possible.

Assessment and Intervention Planning

Based on the information that you collected during the interview, as well as any questionnaire data that you obtain, you complete your intake assessment in one or two sessions. You now compare your information about Chuck with the mental skills that are characteristic of successful elite athletes (discussed in detail in Chapter Four) and develop an intervention plan.

Motivation

Successful elite athletes are aware of the benefits that they expect to experience through sport participation. They have the ability to persist through difficult tasks and difficult times, even when these benefits are not immediately forthcoming.

ASSESSMENT: Both the interview and the MSAF indicate that Chuck is highly motivated to succeed in golf. He has made considerable sacrifices for his sport but believes that they have been worthwhile. The primary reasons that he plays golf, he states on the MSAF, are to have fun, to earn self-respect, and the excitement of competition. He reports a high level of satisfaction on each of these during the past two weeks.

INTERVENTION: None indicated.

Setting and Achieving Goals

Successful, elite athletes are able to set long-term and short-term goals that are realistic, behavioral, measurable, and time oriented. They are able to assess their performance level and develop a specific, detailed plan for attaining their goals. They are able to identify and obtain the resources necessary to achieve the goal.

ASSESSMENT: Chuck has worked closely with his golf pro and his father in establishing both long-term and short-term goals. He intends to become a teaching pro after college and is well informed of the qualifications that he must meet. His current goals are to reduce his average score for this season by three strokes and improve his putting, so that he "2 putts" at 85 percent of the time. He has a clear plan for using his pro and knows what types of practice he needs to engage in.

INTERVENTION: None indicated.

Arousal Control

Successful, elite athletes are able to discover and regulate their optimal state of emotional arousal prior to and during competition.

> Assessment: Chuck is very much aware of the fact that he is unable to control his arousal level both before and during competition. This not only spoils the fun of golf but impairs his performance as well. His anxiety and worry during competition lead to muscle stiffness and loss of fluid movement, necessary for a good shot. Although he knows that he needs to relax, he doesn't know how to do it.
>
> Intervention: Chuck is a good candidate for relaxation training. You decide to conduct two sessions of relaxation training: one on physical relaxation and one on mental relaxation. Each session will be tape-recorded, and Chuck will be instructed to practice his relaxation at home on a daily basis for several weeks. Later he will be instructed to do six to eight mini-relaxations each day using a cue phrase. Next, he'll be instructed to practice these on the golf course during low-stress rounds, then finally during high-stress competitions. You have discovered that Chuck has an excellent preshot routine, so you don't need to address that. Finally, Chuck doesn't have a precompetition routine, so you will help him design one. This will be a standard sequence of behaviors that he will perform during the ten minutes prior to his first tee-off. After using it many times, it will become familiar and comforting to him.

Attention Control

Successful, elite athletes have the ability to develop a precise awareness of what stimuli they need to attend to during a particular game or sport situation. They have the ability to maintain focus on these stimuli and resist all forms of distraction, whether from the environment or from within themselves; to regain focus when it has been lost during competition; and to play in the here-and-now without regard to either past or anticipated future events.

ASSESSMENT: Although Chuck is keenly aware of what he needs to pay attention to at each stage of his game, he feels that he doesn't know how to do this, especially when he feels the pressure of high-level competition. Although he experiences occasional distractions from the environment, his worst distractions come from within himself: his own thoughts about his overall score or previous shots that he missed.

INTERVENTION: After relaxation training is well underway, you will take Chuck through the attention-focusing exercise that will improve his ability to shift between broad and narrow modes of attention. You will also teach him how to block out distracting thoughts by replacing them with previously chosen images. This will be accomplished with specific exercises during your session and recordings to practice at home, combined with some suggested changes in self-talk.

Self-Talk

Successful, elite athletes manage their self-confidence and challenges in a positive, constructive manner through healthy habits of self-talk. Sometimes self-talk is based on cognitive-behavioral strategies for reframing a situation, or simply a cue word selected to elicit specific thoughts, feelings, and behaviors.

ASSESSMENT: One of the major reasons for Chuck's difficulty in letting go of thoughts of his overall score or previous shot is his self-talk. On questioning, you have learned what he typically says to himself in various situations: "Three above par; gonna have to shave a stroke on each of the next two holes in order to finish in the top five." Or, "Can't believe I missed that putt! God, I just can't putt today. I just can't do anything right today. My game is really going down the tubes."

Intervention: Now that you have identified the self-defeating self-talk that typically occurs in specific situations, you can begin to develop more productive statements for Chuck to substitute for these in the future. Instead of thinking about his overall score, suggest such statements as: "One shot at time." Or, "Focus on the upcoming shot." After a poor shot, "Let it go." Or, "Good golfer, poor shot." You will also help him to develop several positive affirmations that he can use during the evening before and the day of competition to help reduce his anxieties.

Emotional Control

Successful, elite athletes are able to control strong emotions—anger, elation, or despondency—when they interfere with performance. These emotional states frequently accompany mistakes and errors or sometimes performing above one's expectations.

Assessment: You ask Chuck to describe in detail the situations in which he becomes angry at himself. Usually this is a situation in which he has missed an easy putt that he believes that he should have made. In addition to critical, negative, global self-talk, he has occasionally displayed this anger publicly by swearing and throwing his club. Both his pro and his father have told him he must learn to control his anger, especially this outward display. In addition to being uncomfortable, anger is usually accompanied by a loss of concentration and further poor performance.

Intervention: First, you will work on Chuck's belief system regarding anger. Many young athletes seem to believe that anger at self is automatic, appropriate, and helpful. You will challenge these assumptions by asking Chuck if his anger causes him to play better. Inevitably, in golf and most other sports, the answer will be a clear no. You will ask Chuck what he'd say to a best friend of similar ability who'd missed that shot. The answer is almost always a positive, supportive one: "I'd tell him to just forget about it." Or, "You're okay. Even pros miss easy shots like that; just play the next shot as best you can." Pretty good. Now it is time for

Chuck to learn to become his own best friend. Several "best friend" statements will be written down on small cards that Chuck can carry with him and use when he misses an easy shot.

If Chuck doesn't respond to this initial simplistic approach, you may decide to work with his anger in a more concerted manner—for example, by exploring other manifestations of anger in his life, how he reacts, and the usual consequences. The focus would be on helping Chuck to develop greater sensitivity to the early signs of anger and an awareness of alternative strategies. You might role-play situations and practice these new behaviors.

Mental Imagery

Successful, elite athletes are able to imagine themselves performing specific behaviors at a high level of excellence clearly and vividly, using multiple sensory modalities: mentally rehearsing situations and performances in advance and dealing with errors and poor performances through mental imagery correction, rather than reliving the mistake mentally.

ASSESSMENT: Upon questioning, as well as on the MSAF, you discover that Chuck uses mental imagery infrequently and mostly in a negative manner after completing a poor shot that he replays over and over again in his mind.

INTERVENTION: Chuck will benefit from developing positive mental imagery skills. After explaining the technique and its rationale, you will begin instructing him how to use this powerful mental tool. Initially, you will ask him to take a moment after an especially good shot to relive it in his mind—a mental replay. Again, imagery should include as many of the senses as possible. You will teach him how to do a mental correction immediately after a poor shot, in order to help let it go and close out the experience on a positive note. After he is successful in imaging small sequences of behavior, you will guide him through imagery of his performing well in a variety of selected golf situations that have been difficult for him. Finally, you may guide him through an entire mental round of golf that incorporates many of the situations and techniques that he has worked on.

Carrying Out the Intervention

Based on the intervention plan that you've developed, you now meet with Chuck once a week. Each session begins with a review of the homework tasks that you assigned and his response. Did he carry out the tasks? What did he experience? What mental tools has he used on the golf course, and what were the results? If he played golf during the week, you also ask him to analyze his play in terms of the mental skills concepts that he has now learned.

At each stage, you are careful to convey realistic expectations about mental skills training. Although you are optimistic about his ability to learn these skills and apply them to golf and other areas of life, you do not expect quick results. As with the golf skills, these skills will take considerable practice both on and off the course. Generally when I begin working with an athlete, I ask her to commit at least fifteen minutes a day every day to developing the mental aspects of the sport.

Your continued dialogue with the client will enable you to refine your intervention strategy as you go along. Some goals may be deleted and others added. Hopefully, the point will be quickly reached when the client experiences the benefits of the mental skills training. When appropriate, sessions may be tapered to once every two or three weeks, before major competition, or simply as needed. As in traditional counseling, clients come with a wide variety of problems, abilities, and expectations. Some pass through the process very quickly. Others will continue for a long time.

ELITE ATHLETES

If you are just beginning to develop sport psychology within your practice, it is unlikely that you will be working with elite athletes, especially for performance-enhancement services. Even with respect to clinical and counseling issues, the lifestyle and the demands of elite athletes are sufficiently different from most of your clinical clients that special understanding and sensitivities will be required. There is no substitute for experience, and the more you cultivate and develop your skills with recreational athletes, the better you'll be equipped to work with elite athletes when the opportunity arises.

Your Own Preparation

You're now progressing in a self-education program, perhaps based on the recommendations in Chapter Two. You have read widely, both books and journals, attended workshops and conferences, and perhaps have even met with a collegial study group on a regular basis. You may have acquired considerable knowledge but limited applied skills, which you know can be acquired only through experience. To develop your skills, then, you need practical experience, and lots of it. Before becoming a full-fledged sport psychologist, you need to "pay your dues" or "toil in the vineyards," as the sayings go.

Working with individual athletes is the building block for developing and refining your practical skills. Individual consultation challenges you to make assessments, plan and implement highly focused interventions, and receive direct feedback that enables you to assess the outcome of your efforts and modify them accordingly. You'll benefit by working with a wide variety of athletes from different sports, as well as representing different ages, genders, and levels of commitment.

Psychological Development of Elite Athletes

Although the personal histories of elite athletes show considerable variations due to their individuality, their families, and their particular sport, there are a sufficient number of common experiences to be worthy of mention. Elite athletes, for example, are likely to have begun their athletic career early in life. Endowed with natural physical and mental attributes and fortunate opportunities, it is likely that their talent manifested at an early age. They may have played and excelled in a variety of sports, but began specializing in one sport at an earlier age than most others. The greater their talent, the more likely it was noticed at an early age and the more it affected their psychological development.

Early Years

As with prodigies in music, art, drama, and other endeavors, the talented child is often excused from customary household and school responsibilities in order to nurture his special talent. The movie *Searching for Bobby Fischer,* based on a true story, is an excellent depiction of the issues facing an unusually talented child and his family—in this case, a chess player but the issues are the same as those of young elite athletes.

One frequently experienced issue is the parents' conflict between "nurturing the special talent" versus "nurturing the whole child" so that he experiences a close-to-normal childhood. The father in the movie favors nurturing the talent, the mother the whole child. This dichotomy brings them into conflict with one another, a conflict that is resolved successfully before the end of the movie.

Such has not been true with the families of several of the young committed and elite athletes I've worked with. In several cases, one parent had been overly involved with the child's sport, to a very unhealthy extreme for all concerned: the involved parent, the spouse, the child, and siblings. It has always been difficult for me to understand whether this over-involvement in the child's sports is the cause or the effect of a dysfunctional marriage, and my efforts to address this situation are usually vigorously rebuffed. On the other hand, I have known very healthy families who have maintained appropriate balance and have successfully nurtured both the talent and the whole child.

The disproportionate amount of attention that the young athlete receives from parents and their willingness to put their own needs aside is a potential source of trouble, especially if not handled properly by the parents. The youngster may develop feelings of entitlement and expectations that his needs are more important than those of others, an attitude that can lead to severe problems now and in the future. If there are siblings, the attention and resources devoted to the prodigy athlete can lead to severe feelings of resentment, which they do not always express in a direct manner.

In order to succeed, the young athlete must pay attention to and nurture his body. He must learn to monitor and regulate physiological processes, such as eating, sleeping, and conditioning, in order to obtain high levels of performance. In order to follow a training program, he must be self-focused and uncompromising. These circumstances, if they are not properly balanced by parental guidance, can lead to the development of a highly self-centered, narcissistic individual. Parents have the difficult responsibility of teaching the young athlete to be sensitive and respectful of others whose lives may not be as focused and goal oriented.

Although the stresses and potential pitfalls may be great, early athletic participation at a high level can provide the child with the potential benefits of good role models, self-respect, healthy excitement, fun, self-confidence, discipline, fitness, stress management skills, positive life values, and positive, shared family experiences.

Adolescence

If the developing elite athlete participates in a school sport that is mainstream and seasonal, such as football, he is likely to receive attention from peers, adults, and local media. These adolescents tend to be popular and may have fairly normal socializing experiences, especially during the off-season. However, they are at risk of being overvalued for their athletic accomplishments and may not develop the healthy give-and-take social skills that are required of their peers and are necessary for healthy social development. When this happens, they may internalize standards of worth based on their athletic performances, which can predispose them to serious personal crises later, when their proficiency diminishes or they are no longer able to participate in their sport.

A few years ago, I worked with a young man who had been expelled from a prestigious college during his freshman year for repeated episodes of intoxication and violent behavior. In high school he had won two state championships as a wrestler and had enjoyed great popularity among his classmates. Once in college, with a substantial scholarship, he became an "alternate" in his weight class and never wrestled in a meet. Depressed by this situation, he stopped his vigorous training, ate poorly, began drinking, and finally was dismissed from the team. This led to an identity crisis and even more drinking. When he started therapy with me after his expulsion, he expressed strong feelings of anger at all those people, including his parents and former high school classmates, who had seen him only as a wrestler and not as a whole person. With so much of his childhood devoted to developing his wrestling skills and having achieved popularity easily, his academic and social skills were severely underdeveloped.

If the developing elite athlete participates in a less popular, non-school sport, such as figure skating, no matter how talented she is, she runs the risk of being unpopular or unknown at school and missing out on many of the normal socializing experiences. This is especially true of year-round sports that require long hours of practice during the school year and out-of-town competitions on weekends. Often friendships, because of limited social opportunities, are restricted to others who participate in the sport. These friendships lack the variety that occurs in a normal school environment and are often shallow because the child's closest friend may also be her fiercest competitor.

"Following the Dream"

By midadolescence or earlier, the developing elite athlete is usually "following the dream." This may be to make an Olympic team, win a gold metal or a national championship, or have a career as a professional athlete. She receives feedback from experts, coaches, officials, and scouts that the dream is obtainable and that she has natural talent. She will have to cultivate that talent through hard work, discipline, and dedication to long-term goals. Often additional resources are needed to pursue the dream to the fullest. Parents may spend considerable money on equipment, summer camps, special coaches, training workshops, sports medicine specialists, and even sport psychologists. Often this entails travel or living away from home for extended periods of time. Spontaneity becomes the exception, as the child's life is directed by demands and schedules.

When the family's financial resources are limited, parents may seek sponsors to help defray the costs, professionals who will work without pay, and schools that will provide scholarships in exchange for being affiliated with and contributing to a future champion. For example, the movie *Hoop Dreams* depicts the struggle of two disadvantaged inner-city youths with dreams of playing NBA basketball.

Obligation to Others

Consuming a disproportionate amount of resources from family, coaches, and others, the young elite athlete usually feels an obligation to perform well, even when this is not directly asked of him. There may be a strong desire to please those who have sacrificed so much. If he becomes burned out or considers dropping out in order to pursue other interests, he is unlikely to act on these thoughts because of a strong sense of obligation. Sometimes injuries provide a face-saving way of temporarily or permanently leaving the sport and its pressures.

During performance slumps, the aspiring elite athlete feels a tremendous pressure to perform, not just for himself but for others whom he doesn't want to "let down." It's an unusual elite athlete who reaches a level of maturity that enables him to rise above all of these pressures and "play for himself," with no feelings of obligation to others. Rarely does this occur early in an athlete's career.

College Years

If college is in the career path of the developing elite athlete, the college experience will be quite different from that of most other college students. The selection of the college, academic major, living situation, class schedule, and social contacts will be greatly influenced by sport career decisions. Some of the aspects of the high school situation, especially with respect to popularity and media publicity, will be even greater in college when the sport is mainstream. At this level, sport priorities take precedence over academics, especially when the goal is a lucrative professional sport career. Sport participation will be extremely demanding of the athlete's time and energies, with long practices and travel to away games.

Developmentally, this is a difficult time for the elite athlete. At a time when it is normal and desirable for young people to be expanding their range of interests, knowledge, and experiences, the constraints of athletic participation lead the elite athlete to narrow his attention to his sport and places severe limits on his academic and social life. In both areas, he has less time for these aspects of life and is also less likely to have the full variety of experiences that his nonathletic counterpart enjoys. Many colleges, aware of these pressures, provide counseling programs geared to the special needs of their athletes.

Resolution of "the Dream"

Although the timing may differ according to each sport, sooner or later the "dream" either becomes a reality, or it becomes clear that it will not be fulfilled. Since there are fewer and fewer positions at each successive level of the sports pyramid and competition for these positions is fierce, the majority of aspiring elite athletes will not fulfill their dream. If they have maintained perspective, developed other marketable skills, and learned life lessons from their sport participation, they will redirect their energies toward alternative healthy goals. Those who have not done so are at great risk of experiencing personal crises and need strong support from friends, family, and possibly a professional counselor who is knowledgeable about their life path and current crisis.

Achieving or living the dream does not automatically lead to happiness or all of the envisaged consequences. Olympians, for example, even those who have won gold or silver medals, sometimes experience a tremendous letdown after the games. After a few weeks of media attention, life goes back to normal all too quickly. There may be loss of purpose as the goal that has guided the athlete's life for years is gone, and no new goal has taken its place. This is especially true for athletes in sports without a professional level to move up to. On top of this may be the disappointments that jobs, product endorsements, and other financial rewards that were anticipated have not materialized. The athlete may wonder whether these few minutes in the sun were worth the years of sacrifice.

The Professional Athlete

If "living the dream" means entering a higher level of competition, such as becoming a professional athlete in a major league sport, the athlete now enters a whole new world of changes, benefits, and pressures. At the time of signing a contract, the athlete may become instantly wealthy, a situation for which he is totally unprepared. Suddenly his life and everything about it becomes highly visible, both on and off the playing field or court. Relocating, frequent travel, long hours, adjustment to new team members, and separation from family, friends, and support system are only a few of the major changes that the new professional must cope with. Additionally, there is the adjustment of dealing with friendly, but intrusive, fans, as well as critical and hostile fans, both in and out of the arena.

With the transition to the professional level, the sport itself may be experienced differently. Other players, both teammates and opponents, are of a much higher caliber than before. Practices are longer, games are tougher, the season is longer, and games are scheduled close together without as much time for recovery. The consequences of poor performance are much greater and much more public. In this world of contracts and agents, earnings may be secure for a limited time, but the player is "owned" by the team and may be traded with no warning because of poor performance, good performance, or reasons not readily apparent.

Once having arrived on the professional scene, the athlete lives in a fiercely competitive world in which his performance, productivity, and worth are constantly under scrutiny by his owners, coaches, teammates, fans and media. Performance slippage attracts significant attention and compounds worry and an inappropriate negative focus. Every performance is measured and contributes to weekly, seasonal, and career statistics that are not only compared to teammates and competitors but to everyone else who has ever played the game.

For those who enter this world immature, there are the temptations of the fast life, quick gratification of most needs enabled by their instant wealth, readily available sex and adoration, and easy access to alcohol, gambling, and drugs.

Even when all is going well, the professional athlete lives with the ever-present risk that sudden injury could temporarily interrupt or prematurely end his career. In spite of a common tendency to deny, there is also the reality that the aging process will eventually lead to a decline in performance and ultimately to retirement from the sport.

In spite of the many stresses, the life of the professional athlete can also be a highly rewarding one. At each stage of development, there are opportunities to develop mental skills through sports that can be applied to other areas of life as well. The potential for self-actualization, recognition from others, doing something that one loves, and the financial remuneration can lead to a satisfying and rewarding lifestyle.

Working with Elite Athletes

Halfway through the season, Bart, a major league baseball veteran of twelve years, was in a hitting slump. Although he had experienced this before, this one was different. In the past he had been able to shrug it off, and it never lasted long. Now it persisted; he was becoming preoccupied with the problem and had difficulty relaxing or sleeping at night. Although his manager gave him reassurances to the contrary, rumors in the clubhouse, as well as in the media, indicated that he was about to be traded to a West Coast team within the next few days. At home he had become worried about his wife's increased drinking and his adolescent daughter's remarks that she'd "rather die" than move again. With all of this on his mind, it was difficult to concentrate and play baseball.

At every stage of development, the elite athlete lives in an unusual world with high levels of pressure from within himself and from others. The risks are great; so are the benefits. Some of the psychological characteristics of the elite athlete may be familiar to you if you've worked with other highly focused, achievement-oriented clients who have reached high levels of excellence and recognition in their fields.

There are numerous times and situations, from early childhood through retirement, in which elite athletes may find themselves psychologically stressed and in need of counseling. Particularly during the formative years, the sport psychologist can play an important role in helping the parents of the young athlete to find a healthy balance between nurturing the whole child and nurturing the talent and the rest of the family. Additionally, the sport psychologist may help the family achieve a healthy balance in addressing the needs of each of its members.

In the case of Bart, for example, in addition to individual sessions with him, I also met with him, his wife, and his daughter on several occasions. Each of the three had reacted to the possible move individually, without sharing thoughts and feelings with the others. During the family sessions, the focus was on formulating a family plan for dealing with relocation that would take into account the needs of each member. Bart was not traded during the several months that I worked with him and slowly came out of his slump. As it turned out, his wife's drinking was not as great a problem as he had imagined it to be. His daughter promised to express her disapproval of moving in a less dramatic way, as long as her parents would to listen to her. They readily agreed to this.

In working with elite athletes, it is important to be mindful of the professional issues of confidentiality and maintaining boundaries. If confidentiality is especially important to a high-profile, easily identified athlete, you'll need to discuss this with him and make accommodations such as scheduling appointments so that he'll not be in your waiting room for a long time or seeing him at a time when the office is closed. Because of media insensitivities and the outright viciousness of some talk radio shows, in some circumstances an athlete might be seriously harmed by public knowledge that he is seeing a sport psychologist. This is unfortunate for the athlete, and for our profession, but nevertheless a reality in some circumstances.

The elite athlete, at least in season, may be one of the most heavily scheduled people you'll ever meet. Between team practices and meetings, personal conditioning regimes, public relations work, family, and considerable travel, there is little time remaining. Don't expect the regularity of "every Tuesday at 1:00 P.M." You may have to work on an irregular basis and make yourself available, both in the office and on the telephone, at odd times.

In working with the elite athletes, regardless of their stature, it is important for you to resist being starstruck. Your athlete already has millions of fans and doesn't need another one. He needs a professional, a person to whom he can relate and feel comfortable. If you start feeling and acting like a fan, you'll greatly reduce your rapport and effectiveness. The star athlete is accustomed to people wanting something from him—anything from an autograph, to business endorsement, to a friendship. Expect him to be on guard. It may take some time before you're fully trusted.

As with other athletes, your work with the elite athlete may involve counseling, performance enhancement, or both. If you do performance enhancement, remember that an elite athlete has already learned and practiced many of the mewntal skills that you teach. Be cautious so as not to disrupt those habits that have been cultivated and have served him well over many years. Finding areas for improvement will challenge your assessment and intervention abilities.

Two years ago I was being interviewed on the telephone by a well-known professional athlete who was considering my services. After answering some of the most challenging questions that have ever been put to me by a prospective client, his final and most difficult question was, "So how do you think you could help me?" I honestly replied, "I'm not sure. The high level that you've reached in your sport indicates that you probably know more than 95 percent of what I teach. However, if we can identify and make improvements in the remaining 5 percent, I think it will make an important difference." He made an appointment, and we've been working together ever since.

If you've been following the progressive steps in this book or your own pathway, the time will come when you've substantially increased your knowledge, skills, and credentials in sport psychology. You will have accumulated extensive hands-on experience with a wide variety of athletes and situations. At this point, you are ready to expand and market your sport psychology practice, the subject of the final chapter.

8

Marketing Your Sport Psychology Practice

B y now you've probably realized that the possibilities for developing sport psychology within your practice are limited only by your own imagination, ambition, and willingness to work hard. You've also come to realize that there is no clear pathway and that you'll have to make your own way. Now it's time to put it all together: time to focus on your goals, define your sport psychology practice, and begin marketing to your potential clients.

DEFINING YOUR PRODUCT

Before you begin marketing, you need to decide what you're marketing. There are two major approaches to this issue: one I call the *expert* approach, the other the *product* approach. Using the expert approach, you communicate your knowledge, skills, and accomplishments to potential clients, who then, you hope, will hire your services ("rent a brain," you might say). We're familiar with this approach from our academic experience where positions are filled largely through the format of the curriculum vita and its elaborations. In sport psychology, the expert approach works most effectively when the potential client is already knowledgeable about sport psychology and knows what he is looking for. Because we are a new field, however, this will rarely be the case except for those few clients who have already worked with sport psychologists—usually elite-level athletes and some college and professional teams.

One of my many early mistakes was to market my sport psychology services using this expert approach. I presented my background, credentials, experience, and accomplishments and assumed that potential clients would instantly understand how I could help them. What seemed obvious to me was apparently obscure to them. At best, I probably left them with the impression, "Boy, that guy sure knows his stuff." But they didn't have the foggiest idea of how I could help them and rarely called to make appointments. When I realized what was happening, I regrouped and organized my marketing efforts into strategies that I now label a *product approach*.

The particular products that you develop should reflect your own goals. For example, if one of your goals is to get out of the office, you might consider doing on-site workshops or consulting with a high school sports team. If your goal is to maintain your income level but reduce your number of hours, you might develop workshop programs.

Reviewing and Refining Your Goals

Begin by reviewing the goals that you wrote for your practice after reading Chapter One. Have they changed as you have read this book? Can your goals be rewritten more specifically now?

• *Overall practice goals.* Overall, how would you like your practice to be different in the future? In what ways will sport psychology enable you to reshape your practice? How will you measure success? Personal satisfaction? Increased income? Number of hours scheduled? When you work? Where you work? Professional contributions? Peer recognition?

• *Professional activities.* What portion of your professional time do you want to devote to individual consultations? Group and family sessions? Conducting workshops for clients? Conducting workshops for professional colleagues? Research? Writing? Teaching? Presenting at professional conferences? Supervision? Continuing education?

- *Clientele.*   What proportion of your clientele would you like to be regular clinical clients using your usual interventions? Regular clinical clients using your usual interventions plus exercise and sport psychology techniques? Athletes who are referred mostly for counseling or psychotherapy? Athletes who are referred mostly for performance enhancement? Young athletes? Families of young athletes? Coaches? Women athletes? Older athletes? Injured athletes? Recreational athletes? Committed and elite athletes? Athletes with special problems such as eating disorders and substance abuse? Athletes dealing with specific issues such as adjusting to transitions, upward or downward, voluntary or involuntary retirement from sport? Athletes from specific sports (such as golf, gymnastics, skiing, baseball)?

- *Expected rewards.*   What do you expect to experience if you accomplish your goals? Greater job satisfaction? Escape from the tyranny of managed care? Working outside your office? Increased income? Helping others more effectively? Fame? Greater self-respect? Respect and recognition from others? Personal growth? Better personal balance? Having more fun?

- *Intensity of your effort.*   What price are you willing to pay for the attainment of your goals? Work harder? Work longer? Financial sacrifices? Travel? Relocate? How long are you willing to make these sacrifices?

Now that your goals have been defined, you can begin developing specific products that will move you toward attaining them. Consider which services you now provide that are consistent with your goals and which entirely new products you will have to develop.

Product Definition

Think about all of the sport psychology, client-oriented services that you now offer or will offer in the near future. See if you can place them into several logical categories, and then write a short description of each. For example, almost all of my sport psychology direct services fall into one of the following categories, each described as follows in my printed public relations and advertising materials:

• *Individual performance counseling.*   Evaluation of the athlete's current mental skills, development and implementation of an individual plan to improve specific mental skills. Sessions are one-on-one.

• *Adjustment counseling.*   Individual sessions for athletes, members of their families, coaches, and staff who may be experiencing emotional, behavioral or relationship difficulties. Problems may or may not be directly related to sports participation. When appropriate, sessions may include others, such as family members.

• *Seminars and workshops.*   Group educational programs for athletes, parents, and coaches focused on specific topics. Small seminars may be conducted at the Center or on-site for specific groups. Programs are specifically designed to meet the needs of the group.

• *Team consultation.*   Consultation with team managers, coaches, staff, and players regarding morale, communications, and team building.

• *Referrals.*   When necessary, we evaluate and refer clients to other appropriate treatment professionals and facilities. Our referral list includes sports medicine specialists in nutrition, physical therapy, and orthopedics, as well as mental health specialists in eating disorders and substance abuse.

- *Speakers' Bureau.* We can provide a speaker for school, civic, or athletic groups on many subjects regarding mental and emotional aspects of sports. Our speakers include the director, part-time associates of the Center, and professional colleagues.

Once defined, these product descriptions can be used in numerous ways. For example, in a practice brochure, you would probably include a brief description of each, such as that given above. On the other hand, if you are targeting high school coaches for marketing your seminars and workshops, you might expand that specific product description to one page and present it as a stand-alone document.

Professional Identity

All of your sport psychology products should be identified to the public in a manner that is simple, clear, and easily remembered. Corporations use trade names and logos in order to establish this identity, and I suggest you do the same. After promoting my private practice as Jack J. Lesyk, Ph.D., Inc., Clinical & Sport Psychology, for many years, in 1993, after considerable reflection, I decided to market the sport psychology aspect of the practice separately as the Ohio Center for Sport Psychology. A new logo was designed for the center, as well as separate business cards, letterhead stationery, and other materials. What I realized is that it was much more effective to market sport psychology without the close association to clinical psychology and that an organizational name presented a stronger image. The image that I want to project emphasizes the educational rather than the clinical functions of the organization.

This is a judgment call, and you may decide differently. Nevertheless, give considerable thought to your professional identity. Once you've chosen it, it will be difficult to change. Use it in all of your advertising, handouts, memos, stationery, and other material. Give it high visibility and have it associated with the qualities that you want it to evoke in the minds of the public and your potential clients.

CREATING YOUR
MARKETING PACKAGE

Effective marketing materials take time to develop. You never know in advance when a marketing opportunity will present itself, so it's a good idea to be prepared. I have a set of stock items I have developed and retained over the years that are ready for instant use when opportunities arise. Most are kept in a large, looseleaf notebook and are camera ready in order to be photocopied or printed on short notice.

- *Practice brochure.* This is the centerpiece of all your advertising and public relations efforts. Although you may have a combined brochure that covers both your clinical and sport psychology services, I suggest a separate sport psychology brochure. A brochure is an excellent way for a prospective client to see a picture of you and read your words. You start becoming a person, not just a name.

  Consider hiring a public relations expert to design the brochure. This doesn't have to be an exorbitant expense. Often you can find an experienced freelancer who can design and produce camera-ready artwork for less than a thousand dollars. Maybe this sounds like a lot, but it is a worthwhile investment.

  The brochure should be attractive and inviting to read. Use the logo, colors, and photographs to reinforce your identity. Basically the brochure should provide information about whom you serve, what products you provide, how clients benefit, and how you are qualified. It should make your potential clients perceive you as relevant to their concerns, accessible to them, and affordable.

- *Short professional biography.* Although this may be contained in your practice brochure, it is also useful to have it available as a one-page separate item. If you're giving a talk, a brief biography is useful for the person who will introduce you. It makes that person's job easier, and your audience hears the information that you have selected. This is also a good item to give to anyone from the media who has interviewed you. It helps the person get your name, affiliation, and credentials right.

• *Prepared one-hour talk.* Speaking engagements are an excellent way to develop visibility in your community. Put together an interesting one-hour talk that you can give on short notice. Over the years, I have developed several talks for different audiences, most accompanied by slides.

• *Topical handouts.* Prepare a one-page handout on a specific topic that may be distributed when you give a talk, mailed to interested parties, and made available in your waiting room. Some of the topics that I hand out are, "What Is Sport Psychology?" and "A Few Words for Parents and Coaches: Giving Emotional Support to Your Young Athletes." These should contain practical information. The handouts are printed on letterhead stationery so that readers may easily contact me with questions or a referral.

• *Articles you have written.* Keep copies of any articles that you have written for nonprofessional readers to mail to potential clients or distribute when you give talks. If the article has been published, this will add even more to your credibility.

• *Newspaper and magazine clippings.* Articles about you and your professional activities and articles in which you have been quoted help to establish your credibility.

• *Stock advertisements.* Prepare several standard-sized camera-ready advertisements to use for newspapers, newsletters, magazines, and sporting event programs. Sometimes opportunities arise quickly, and you won't have time to design an ad.

- *Testimonials.* Collect quotable statements from credible sources who know your work and endorse it. These statements may be from professional colleagues, coaches, parents, athletes, and workshop participants. For ethical reasons, it is essential that these do not violate any principles of confidentiality and that the client was not pressured or exploited into giving the endorsement. The testimonials I use have been volunteered by clients, usually after our professional work has been concluded.

With all of these materials at your fingertips, you can respond quickly and professionally to requests for information. For example, if a potential client calls me but is not yet ready to make an appointment, I ask for an address so that I can mail information to the person. With ten minutes and a photocopy machine, I can prepare an impressive information packet containing my practice brochure, business card, and copies of articles and handouts relevant to the person's interest and sport. Additionally, reprints of articles I've written and newspaper articles about my work help to establish a perception of professional credibility and competence. Finally, I include a brief, handwritten note (rather than a form letter) thanking her for her interest and requesting that she call me if she has any questions or wishes to make an appointment. The note is deliberately handwritten to make it personal and to suggest that my services will be personalized as well.

The package is usually mailed the same day and often received the following day. Once it is mailed, I don't follow up with a telephone call because I don't want to be perceived as a high-pressure person. In fact, this is unnecessary. Approximately 90 percent of those who receive the package call for an appointment within a day or two.

Responding quickly is important. Often a recent event has prompted the immediate call for professional help, but the problem may have persisted for years. If the potential client is not responded to quickly, the motivation for obtaining help may pass. Additionally, a quick response tells the potential client that he is important.

The same type of package can be quickly assembled for inquiries regarding workshops and seminars as well as media appearances.

Creating Your Professional Image

As a professional, your most important qualities, competence and caring, are inner qualities that the public or your potential client cannot see. They can only be inferred and judged by the appearances that you present, that is, your professional image. Since this image is so important, give serious thought to what you present to others and how you would like to be perceived.

All of your choices say something about you. What image do you want to create in the minds of the public and potential clients? Here is my own answer to this question: I want a new client who walks into my office for the first time to have a feeling that she has already been here and has met me before. She will arrive excited with positive expectations that will be subsequently fulfilled. There will be few questions or doubts, because these have been addressed before her arrival. Everything in this environment will contribute to a feeling that she belongs here and that she will be treated with respect and dignity at all times. She will know that she is working with a caring, fully qualified professional who has experience as an athlete and who believes that sports are important only to the extent that they contribute to the overall joy and balance in a person's life. Although the environment conveys professionalism, it is also warm and informal, making her feel comfortable and safe to discuss her concerns.

I keep these images in mind as I prepare an ad, create a slide presentation, choose my clothing for the day, or speak with a potential client on the telephone. These images guide the content and tone of the products that speak for me.

Consider some of the important tangibles that you can use to enable your new or potential client to create an accurate, positive, intended image of you and your professional services:

• *Printed materials.* Your office brochure, special workshop flyers, business cards, and letterhead may be the items that introduce you to a new person and begin to create an impression. Do not leave the impression to chance. What type of impression do you wish to create? Are your materials successful in creating this impression?

• *Telephone answering.* The next contact point for the new or potential client is likely to be a telephone call to your office. How is your telephone answered? Is the receptionist or answering service representing you the way you want? Ask a few friends to call, and see what impression they get. I prefer to use a voice-mail system. My outgoing message is carefully worded, and the tone of my voice is intended to be professional yet warm. When a message is left, I am automatically paged, and I return the call as quickly as possible. My quick response is intended to say several things to the prospective client: "If we work together, you can count on me to be there for you. Your needs are important, and I will respond to them quickly."

• *Office location.* Your location and address send a message. Within each city are areas commonly viewed as the low-rent district, or upscale, or moderate, or something else. You will want to be convenient to the people you serve and should choose a location that they will find accessible and comfortable. My own advice is to avoid extremes, either of which can scare potential clients away. Their reasons may be irrational, but nevertheless they act on them. For example, they may think that you're not affordable if your office is in a certain upscale office park. Your rates may be exactly the same as everyone else's, but they'll never call to find out.

• *Ambiance*. Your waiting room, furniture, decorations, magazines, and bulletin boards provide information that the potential client will use to make inferences about you, so make sure that you avoid anything that raises questions or doubt. For example, I have always resented physicians who have two-year-old issues of *Time* magazine in their waiting rooms, with their home addresses cut out. This makes me feel as if I am getting scraps from the table and my needs and feelings are not important to them. Dirt, clutter, and damaged or frayed furniture all create a negative impression and raise such questions as, "Doesn't he care about his clients?" Or even worse, "If his waiting room and office are shabby, maybe his work is too."

• *Your office*. This is where most of your client contact will occur. I want clients to feel comfortable in this setting and also know that we are here for a serious purpose. Since I spend a lot of time in this room, I want it to be comfortable for me as well. My decor is sports oriented, but not so athletic as to make my clinical clients feel that they are in the wrong place. I have the usual certificates on the wall, but not too many of them. A large lithograph of the Boston Marathon, a personal memento, and a composite of historic Olympic posters are on the walls. Additionally, a quilt hanging on one wall adds a touch of softness to the room, as well as sound absorption.

• *Personal appearance*. Your personal appearance will affect your new client's impression of you. Once again, think about how you want to be perceived. Do your hair style, clothing, and posture support or distract from that image? Do you appear fit and athletic? Again, there are many positive alternative ways of expressing your individuality. Most important is to correct anything that would lead the client to question whether you are competent and caring. Sometimes it's smart to adjust your manner of dress to be more effective with specific clientele. For example, when I'm conducting a first session with a young athlete, I may dress more casually than usual to distinguish myself from schoolteachers and to establish closer rapport.

Developing a Marketing Plan

Now that you've defined your products, established an identity, and created your marketing tools, it's time to put these elements together with a marketing plan. The plan may be very simple or very elaborate. Since you already have a clinical practice, which is probably consuming much of your time, a simple but focused plan may be adequate for now. As your skills and involvement in sport psychology develop, the marketing plan can evolve as well.

As with other professional activities, first decide on the amount of resources that you're willing to devote to marketing. How many hours per week? How many dollars per month? To what extent do you need advice and professional assistance from others? What results do you expect? How will you evaluate the results of your efforts? When will you move on to the next set of marketing activities?

Resist the tendency to be all things to all people. Although you may want to develop a full and comprehensive range of services in sport psychology, do so one step at a time. In my marketing, I use a two-track approach. The first track is intended to establish my credentials as a generalist—someone who has a wide variety of psychology and sport psychology experiences (many sports, different ability levels, many types of programs and services). This helps establish credibility and trust in my competence. It also suggests that although I may have not worked with her particular sport or circumstances, I can generalize from my experiences and be effective with her (which I think is usually accurate).

The second track of the plan is focused on developing specific types of referrals. Usually this is for a limited period of time and changes periodically. For example, at one time my major focus was in developing referrals from the equestrian community. During that phase I attended horse shows, conferred with trainers, both on site and in my office, ran low-cost workshops, and advertised in a local equestrian newsletter. As these efforts became successful, I gradually reduced the intensity of these marketing activities and shifted my focus to another area. Once established, maintenance of referrals from a given area is not difficult. For example, I still advertise in the equestrian publication, maintain contact with trainers, and attend horse shows, but not as intensively as before.

A good beginning, then, is to focus on a particular group for marketing your sport psychology services. Based on your goals, knowledge and skills, existing contacts, sport experience, and community need, choose an area to begin. It may be a sport group, such as runners, tennis players, or golfers. Or it may be an "issues" group, such as injured athletes, parents of young athletes, athletes with eating disorders, athletes approaching transition or retirement, or women athletes. What specific services or products do you want to offer? Individual consultation? Workshops? My suggestion is to talk to respected members of the targeted group and plan several workshops or presentations. These are easy to publicize and give the targeted group a low-cost, low-commitment introduction to you and your services. If you are successful, individual referrals will follow.

If you're just starting out, there will probably be a long lag between your efforts and the results. You may be spending considerable time giving talks, for little or no compensation and with few immediate referrals. Be patient. It's not unusual for me when I ask new clients how they became aware of my services to discover that they heard me speak over a year ago or had kept a newspaper clipping from several years ago.

Above all, remember that every contact with every client will always be your most effective marketing activity. In the end, the vast majority of my referrals, both clinical and sport, have always come by word of mouth, from a current or former client's recommending me to a friend or colleague.

MASS MEDIA MARKETING

There are two distinct types of marketing activities aimed at increasing your referrals. The first, using mass media, is a broad-band approach, like a shotgun, aimed at a very wide, public audience, with few likely hits. Your goal is to establish the visibility of sport psychology, your services, and your expertise in the community. The second approach is marketing narrowly to targeted groups such as figure skaters, golfers, or injured athletes. Each approach enhances the effectiveness of the other, and sometimes they may overlap.

In the mass media approach, you broadcast your message to a wide and diverse general audience. Your goal is for a large number of people to learn a few facts about you and your professional activities. Four important points should be emphasized: (1) your professional identity, (2) the athletes you serve, (3) how they benefit, and (4) how you can be contacted.

For the most part, mass media advertising is expensive and has a relatively low yield rate of new referrals. Sport psychology is a high-end, limited product with a small number of potential consumers. Thus, a mass marketing advertising approach is not likely to be cost-effective. Nevertheless, don't ignore this avenue entirely because mass media provide an excellent opportunity for publicity or exposure that costs you nothing. Such exposure strengthens your image and credibility more than any advertising that you can purchase. Here are my frank recommendations on some of the commonly used mass media modalities for advertising and publicity:

- *Newspaper advertising.* For the most part this is expensive and not worthwhile, especially in large metropolitan areas where rates are high. Good advertising requires frequent repetition, which will drive the costs up even further. If you do use newspaper ads, use them for a specific workshop or seminar and advertise it repeatedly during the weeks prior to the scheduled time. Better yet, consider using weekly suburban papers or community guides where rates are lower and you can target a specific geographic area.

- *Yellow Pages.*   Don't spend a lot of money on a large, expensive ad. I have done that and regretted it. Do place an appropriate, modest ad that tells the public that you are practicing sport psychology or performance-enhancement services (whatever words are appropriate to your profession). My listing in the Yellow Pages is modest but attracts enough referrals to make it worthwhile.

- *Radio and television talk shows.*   This sounds like a good opportunity and might turn out to be one; however, these shows are usually on the air at a time when most people are working, and you may not reach your targeted audience. Local television and radio stations are always looking for new guests, so it may not be difficult to get on these shows. Consider one disadvantage: this is an entertainment medium, and hosts usually want you to say outrageous things and give personality interpretations of notable sports figures. Since I refuse to do either of these, my entertainment value is limited, and I prefer to avoid this modality.

Along these lines, I've also made it a policy not to discuss the personality or psychological issues of any named athletes, whether or not I've worked with them. Nor do I respond to any questions about whether I have worked with a named athlete. My response to such questions is brief: "I never confirm or deny working with a specific athlete for reasons of professional confidentiality." Again, this is the opposite of what the media usually want. They want you to "analyze" a particular athlete, especially one you have worked with.

Several times I have been invited by local television stations to be interviewed about the psychological makeup of former Cleveland's Indians baseball player Albert Belle. Each time I refused but offered instead to discuss the pressures of major league professional athletes, how they deal with them, and what we can learn from this.

They politely withdrew their invitations. Ironically, on several occasions other psychologists, who don't even practice sport psychology (fortunately) have accepted these invitations and gone on these shows to give interpretations of Belle's personality and why his anger is so easily provoked.

• *Radio or television brief interviews.*   Usually these opportunities are related to a news story and require little of your time, so there is not much cost to you. For example, several times I've been asked to comment on local sporting news events, such as Cleveland's football fans' reaction to the loss of the Browns. Radio stations tape an interview on the telephone, and television stations send a reporter and cameraperson to your office. Although you may only get twenty seconds of airtime, it is usually repeated on the news several times when there is a large, general audience. This is a long shot for new referrals, but it does happen, and it serves as well to increase the credibility of your expertise in the field.

But be prepared for disappointment. You may give a television station a half-hour interview and find it cut to fifteen seconds (and not even your most profound fifteen seconds) or, worse yet, cut entirely.

If you are contacted by these media for an interview, respond quickly. They have tight production schedules, and if you are unavailable to be interviewed within an hour or two, they'll look for someone else.

• *Newspaper and magazine quotes.*   Most of what I've said about television and radio interviews applies to newspaper and magazine interviews. Fortunately the time urgency is usually not quite as great, but most reporters need their information within a day or two. The advantage of this medium is that you can add the article to your portfolio and use copies of it in your marketing efforts. Again, be prepared to be cut to a short statement or not appear in the article at all.

You may decide to be active in getting media coverage. It is possible to call a radio or television station and speak to the person who selects and schedules guests for talk shows. Cite your credentials and offer to discuss specific topics that you believe have audience appeal—for example, "the changing role of women in sports" and "helping your children benefit from their sports participation." Follow up with a letter and written materials that substantiate your credibility and expertise. Indicate your interest and availability for news-related stories as well. For example, I've been asked for brief comments when the Cleveland Indians lost the World Series in 1995 and when popular quarterback Bernie Kosar was unexpectedly dismissed from the Cleveland Browns in 1993. Also remember to notify your local professional association and referral service that you are practicing sport psychology since this is how media representatives identify experts on particular topics.

Finally, send out press releases when you participate in a special event, such as giving a presentation or conducting a workshop. At the least, you may get a free listing on one of their events calendars. Or you may end up with a full story.

Several years ago, I sent out a press release announcing a mental skills training workshop for equestrians to a suburban newspaper with a large circulation. A few days later, I was called by a reporter whose newspaper subsequently published a large photograph and a half-page article on my work with equestrians and other athletes. The free publicity was worth thousands of dollars. Ironically, the workshop itself attracted only six participants and was not one of my greatest successes. The newspaper article, on the other hand, generated many referrals during the following months and to this day remains an important item in my portfolio.

FOCUSED MARKETING

In the focused marketing approach, your communications are aimed narrowly at carefully selected or targeted groups of potential clients. These may be sports groups such as golfers, gymnasts, and equestrians, or they may be groups defined by a common interest or issue such as parents of young athletes, injured athletes, or women in sports.

The first step is selecting such a group. This choice should be based on your expertise as well as marketing opportunities. You may choose a sport that you've participated in, one in which you've already worked with many athletes, or one that has good market potential because of high numbers of participants who are likely to be aware of a need for your services.

Organization

Once you've picked the sport, and before developing a marketing plan, you need to find out about the organizational structure of that sport. For example, although figure skaters may practice at several different rinks, when they compete, they must represent a figure skating club. In my area there are twelve such clubs. Since I discovered that, I market in a more specific, focused manner. Both coaches and skaters teach and practice at different rinks, so there is some feeling of community between those with different club affiliations. I can, for example, conduct a skating workshop at one club and attract enrollments from other clubs. Equestrians, on the other hand, have very strong affiliations with their barns, which is where they board their horses and do all of their training. There is considerable rivalry, and even jealousy, between those affiliated with different barns, so I work with them one at a time. If you do a workshop at one barn, even though it's open to members of other barns, don't expect the outsiders to come. Neutral sites don't draw impressive numbers either.

The best way to discover the organizational structure of a sport is to ask participants and coaches. Sometimes this seems so obvious to them that they will have some difficulty in explaining it. Even if you have to dig a little for this information, do not omit this important stage in marketing.

Let us examine some of the ways to market to specific targeted groups.

Coaches

Coaches are a good source of potential referrals if you cultivate your relationship with them carefully. When I'm working with an athlete from an individual sport, such as figure skating, gymnastics, or riding, I ask the client's permission to speak with their coach. They usually supply it. When possible, I visit the coach in his setting and summarize my assessment and intervention plan for the athlete. I solicit his suggestions, as well as his support, and usually obtain both easily. My goal is to begin a relationship that I can nurture and develop.

Most coaches in individual sports have been very accepting and positive to this approach. They seem to grasp that I'm an asset to them, not a competitor. In these sports, the coaches know that their income depends on attracting and retaining students. If a particular coach's student has been competing poorly for a period of time, he or she risks losing the student and income to another coach. Thus, if you can help the student perform better, the coach benefits. Developing a positive, trusting relationship with such a coach can be a longtime source of future referrals. Observing coaches teaching and asking them questions are also excellent ways of increasing your knowledge of the sport.

If there is an association of coaches for a particular sport, find out about it. Most coaches' associations are always looking for interesting speakers for their meetings, and this is another excellent opportunity to introduce yourself and your services. Be sure you have attractive and useful handouts. Volunteer your availability for brief telephone consultations. If this group has a newsletter, see if you can subscribe to it. Or even better yet, ask if you can join the organization, at least as an associate member. For example, I am, as far as I know, the only nonequestrian member of the Ohio Professional Horseman Association (ten dollars a year) and the only non–figure skating coach who has membership in the Cleveland Coaches Counsel (twenty-five dollars a year). My membership in both organizations includes a subscription to a valuable newsletter with useful information, competition schedules, and an opportunity to advertise at a low rate to a focused market.

Coaches of team sports are totally different. They usually feel overworked and have no extra time, especially for concerns about an individual athlete, unless that athlete is one of their stars. They are usually salaried, and their jobs are contingent on successful team performance. If you are looking for team consultation, this is a good avenue, especially if you are getting started and are willing to work for a low fee or volunteer your time.

In many states, coaches of scholastic sports must acquire continuing-education credits in order to maintain their certification. Giving a talk at one of their educational programs is another good way of introducing your services to this group. Find out who sponsors such programs in your area by asking one of the coaches you know. Most coaches are on the mailing lists for these programs, which are often sponsored by sports medicine hospital departments or physical therapy groups that serve young athletes.

Coaching is a highly stressful occupation. Consider developing stress management and counseling services for coaches, either individually or in workshops.

Presentations

Giving presentations and talks to specific audiences is a good way to give you and your sport psychology practice favorable exposure to selected target groups. The possibilities here are almost endless, depending on your particular goals. If you're targeting young athletes and their parents, consider parent-teacher association and booster club meetings. For greater public exposure, give a presentation at a clinic held in conjunction with a large sporting event such as a marathon. You will get your message to the athletes and probably get media coverage as well.

Sports clubs are another source of speaking engagements, and most are always looking for speakers. Consider clubs that are organized around specific sports, such as running, cycling, or tennis, and tailor your presentation to the specifics of that sport. If you are cultivating exercise and fitness clients, offer to give a talk at fitness centers.

If you're targeting injured athletes, consider professional groups that have contact with such athletes, such as pediatricians, family physicians, orthopedic surgeons, trainers, and physical therapists. Also, identify professional practices in sports medicine or hospitals that offer services in this area.

Don't overlook your own local professional organization. Twice in the past ten years, I've presented my sport psychology work to members of the Cleveland Psychological Association at dinner meetings. On both occasions this has led to referrals from colleagues. Ironically, I rarely get clinical referrals from my fellow clinical psychologists. In clinical work we perform many of the same services and are respectfully competitive with one another. However, most of my professional colleagues view sport psychology, and correctly, as an area in which they are neither trained nor qualified and thus are comfortable making referrals to me in this specialty.

I have several prepared talks that I can modify easily to suit the needs of a specific audience. My usual format is a one-hour package. I speak for about forty-five minutes and leave fifteen minutes for discussion and questions and answers. My talk is upbeat, with plenty of short case examples, especially from the audience's sport. I use slides for part of the presentation and do several participation exercises in relaxation and attention focusing.

Several years ago, I rarely charged for giving talks and was delighted for the marketing opportunity. As I've succeeded in developing my sport psychology practice, I often charge an honorarium, depending on the group and its budget. If there is an opportunity to give a talk that will help raise funds for a worthwhile charity, I am pleased to donate my time and services.

Newsletters and Magazines

Sport-specific newsletters and magazines are a good vehicle for addressing targeted groups. Most local clubs have newsletters with low advertising rates. You also could benefit by writing a short article, a series of articles, or a column on sport psychology as applied to that specific sport. About ten years ago I wrote a monthly column for the *Ohio Runner* magazine, called "Running on My Mind." The column was an informal combination of sport psychology and my own reflections on running in my life. Although I didn't seek or receive payment for writing this column, it gave me excellent exposure to the running community and credible reprints for my marketing kit.

Direct Mail

Direct mailing of your practice brochure or a flyer for a specific workshop is another method for reaching members of a targeted group. Mailing lists can be obtained from sports clubs, as well as from newsletter and magazine subscriptions lists. In some cases, you may have to pay a fee for using the lists. Generally this is a fairly high-cost option, with limited return. I've tried it on a few occasions, with no great success.

Advertising in Local Sporting Event Programs

Local horse shows, figure skating competitions, high school sports, and other similar events often publish a program. These publications, although small in circulation, are sold or given away at the event and usually received by a select, limited audience that may coincide with one of your targeted marketing groups. Ads in these publications are usually inexpensive. In addition to generating new referrals, you ad will generate goodwill because you are showing financial support for the sport and identifying yourself with that sport community. A good guideline to remember is "Support the Sport."

Sport-Specific Mental Skills Workshops

Mental skills training workshops can serve as both a product and an effective marketing tool. Workshops can be planned with a wide variety of formats for any number of participants. At one extreme, I've conducted an intensive half-day workshop at a university for sixty long-distance runners and their coaches. At the other extreme, I've run a once-a-week, one-hour, six-session workshop for eight tennis players in my office conference room. My fees for workshops have varied widely, from about thirty-five dollars per participant for large-scale workshops to two hundred dollars per person for enrollment in a six-session workshop with few participants. Whenever working with young athletes, I try to remain sensitive to financial situations that might preclude an interested youngster from attending a workshop and sometimes reduce the fee to a token amount. Usually the school coach calls these situations to my attention and is the only one, besides the student and myself, who is aware of the fee adjustment.

Regardless of workshop size, I invite coaches to attend at no cost in order to give them the opportunity to observe for themselves what I do. This has led to goodwill plus unsolicited endorsements and referrals.

Workshops give large numbers of potential clients an opportunity to sample your sport psychology services at a low cost and without commitment. They also tend to reduce the stigma sometimes associated with individual sessions with a sport "shrink," a perception that fortunately seems to be dissipating. Additionally, interactive workshops provide you with an excellent opportunity for learning more about a particular sport, the sport culture, and typically encountered problems.

When I plan a workshop, I usually create a trifold brochure, with pictures of the specific sport as well as a mail-in registration form. The brochures are distributed to appropriate sports clubs, equipment stores, schools, and coaches. To encourage early registration, I offer a free relaxation tape to the first ten registrants, as well as a discount for those who sign up prior to a deadline, usually one week before the workshop. Despite these efforts, it's not unusual to receive a flood of registrations during the last day or two, as well as walk-ins.

From a marketing point of view, workshops can be a newsworthy item for local media coverage, as well as sports and club newsletters. Make sure you send out press releases to a wide variety of media contacts. If you can get an organization, such as a school, running club, university, or charitable organization, to sponsor the workshop, it will use its media and public relations resources to publicize the event for you. With these advantages, you might consider conducting selective workshops at low cost, just for the marketing benefits alone.

The journey of a thousand miles begins with a single step. I hope that the ideas and experiences that I've shared have stimulated you to take that first step. The field of sport psychology is new and growing. You have an opportunity to become a part of it and influence its future and your own too.

Appendix

SELECTED READINGS
IN SPORT PSYCHOLOGY

Introduction and Overview of Sport Psychology

Gill, D. L. (1986). *Psychological dynamics of sport*. Champaign, IL: Human Kinetics.

Horn, T. (1992). *Advances in sport psychology*. Champaign: IL: Human Kinetics.

Murphy, S. M. (Ed.). (1995). *Sport psychology interventions*. Champaign, IL: Human Kinetics.

Singer, R. N., Murphey, M., & Tennant, K. (1993). *Handbook of research on sport psychology*. New York: Macmillan.

Van Raalte, J. L., & Brewer, B. W. (Eds). (1996). *Exploring sport and exercise psychology*. Washington, DC: American Psychological Association.

Weinberg, R., & Gould, D. (1995). *Foundations of sport and exercise psychology*. Champaign, IL: Human Kinetics.

Williams, J. M. (1993). *Applied sport psychology*. Mountain View, CA: Mayfield Publication Co.

Performance Enhancement Techniques

Dalloway, M. (1992). *Visualization: The master skill in mental training*. Phoenix, AZ: Optimal Performance Institute.

Dalloway, M. (1993). *Concentration: Focus your mind, power your game*. Phoenix, AZ: Optimal Performance Institute.

Dalloway, M. (1993). *Drive and determination*. Phoenix, AZ: Optimal Performance Institute.

Dalloway, M. (1993). *Risk taking: Performing your best during critical times.* Phoenix, AZ: Optimal Performance Institute.

Miner, M. J., Shelly, G., & Henschen, A. (1995). *Moving toward your potential: The athlete's guide to peak performance.* Farmington, UT: Performance Publications.

Moran, A. P. (1996). *The psychology of concentration in sport performers: A cognitive analysis.* East Sussex, UK: Psychology Press.

Nideffer, R. M. (1985). *Athlete's guide to mental training.* Champaign, IL: Human Kinetics.

Nideffer, R. M. (1992). *Psyched to win: How to master mental skills to improve your physical performance.* Champaign, IL: Leisure Press.

Orlick, T. (1986). *Psyching for sport: Mental training for athletes.* Champaign, IL: Leisure Press.

Orlick, T. (1990). *In pursuit of excellence: How to win in sport and life through mental training* (2nd ed.). Champaign, IL: Leisure Press.

Porter, K., & Foster, J. (1986). *The mental athlete: Inner training for peak performance.* New York: Ballantine.

Porter, K., & Foster, J. (1990). *Visual athletics: Visualizations for peak sports performance.* Dubuque, IA: Wm. C. Brown.

Sachs, M. L. (1991). Reading list in applied sport psychology: Psychological skills training. *The Sport Psychologist, 5,* 88–91.

Ungerleider, S. (1996). *Mental training for peak performance: Top athletes reveal the mind exercises they use to excel.* Emmaus, PA: Rodale Press.

Mental Skills for Tennis

Gallowey, W. T. (1974). *The inner game of tennis.* New York: Bantam.

Loehr, J. (1991). *The mental game: Winning at pressure tennis.* New York: Penguin Books.

Weinberg, R. S. (1988). *The mental advantage: Developing your psychological skills in tennis.* Champaign, IL: Leisure Press.

Young, B., & Bunker, L. (1994). *The courtside coach: A personal mental trainer for tennis players.* Troy, VA: First Draft Publishing.

Mental Skills for Golf

Fasciana, G. S. (1992). *Golf's mental magic.* Holbrook, MA: Bob Adams.

Gallowey, W. T. (1979). *The inner game of golf.* New York: Random House.

Mackenzie, M. M., & Delinger, K. (1990). *Golf the mind game.* New York: Dell.

Rotella, R., & Bunker, L. (1981). *Mind mastery for winning golf*. New York: Prentice Hall.

Rotella, B. A., & Cullen, B. (1995). *Golf is not a game of perfect*. New York: Simon & Schuster.

Rotella, B., & Cullen, B. (1996). *Golf is a game of confidence*. New York: Simon & Schuster.

Mental Skills for Running

Elliott, R. (1984). *The competitive edge: Mental preparation for distance running*. Englewood Cliffs, NJ: Prentice Hall.

Henderson, J., & Loehr, J. (1991). *Think fast: Mental toughness training for runners*. New York: Penguin Books.

Lynch, J. (1987). *The total runner: A complete guide to optimal performance*. Englewood Cliffs: Prentice Hall.

Sports Rule Books

White, J. R. (Ed.). (1990). *Sports rules encyclopedia* (2nd ed.). Champaign, IL: Leisure Press.

Worth, S. (1990). *Rules of the game*. New York: St. Martin's Press.

Psychological Aspects of Exercise

Berger, B. G. (1994). Coping with stress: The effectiveness of exercise and other techniques. *Quest, 46*(1), 100–119.

Berger, B. G. (1996). Psychological benefits of an active lifestyle: What we know and what we need to know. *Quest, 48*(3), 330–353.

Franks, R. D. (Ed.). (1994). The academy papers: Physical activity and stress [Special issue]. *Quest, 46*(1).

Gill, D. L. (Ed.). (1996). The academy papers: Quality of life: Through movement, health, and fitness [Special issue]. *Quest, 48*(3).

Hafen, B., Karren, K., Frandsen, K., & Smith, N. L. (1996). *Mind/body health: The effects of attitudes, emotions, and relationships*. Boston: Allyn & Bacon.

Hays, K. F. (1993). The use of exercise in psychotherapy. In L. VanderCreek, S. Knapp, & T. L. Jackson (Eds.), *Innovations in clinical practice: A source book* (Vol. 12, pp. 155–168). Sarasota, FL: Professional Resource Press.

Hays, K. F. (1994). Running therapy: Special characteristics and therapeutic issues of concern. *Psychotherapy, 31*(4), 725–734.

Hays, K. F. (1995). Psychotherapy and exercise behavior change. *Psychotherapy Bulletin, 30*(3), 29–35.

International Society of Sport Psychology. (1992). Physical activity and psychological benefits: A position statement. *The Sport Psychologist, 6,* 199–203.

Leith, L. M. (1994). *Foundations of exercise and mental health.* Morgantown, WV: Fitness Information Technology.

Morgan, W. P. (Ed.). (1997). *Physical activity and mental health.* Washington, DC: Taylor & Francis.

Morgan, W. P., & Goldston, S. E. (Eds.). (1987). *Exercise and mental health.* Washington, DC: Hemisphere.

Morrow, J. R., & Gill, D. (Eds.) (1995). The academy papers: The role of physical activity in fitness and health [Special issue]. *Quest, 43*(3).

Sachs, M. L., & Buffone, G. W. (Eds.) (1997). *Running as therapy: An integrated approach.* Northvale, NJ: Jason Aronson.

U.S. Department of Health and Human Services. (1996). *Physical activity and health: A report of the surgeon general* (Order Processing Code 7895). Superintendent of Documents, P.O. Box 371954, Pittsburgh, PA 15250–7954.

Counseling Athletes

Division of Counseling. American Psychological Association. (1993). Sport psychology [Special issue]. *Counseling Psychologist, 21*(3).

Petitpas, A. J. (1996). Counseling interventions in applied sport psychology. In J. L. Van Raalte & B. Brewer (Eds.), *Exploring sport and exercise psychology* (pp. 189–204). Washington, DC: American Psychological Association.

Taylor, J., & Schneider, B. (1992). The sport-clinical protocol: A comprehensive interviewing instrument for applied sport psychology. *Professional Psychology: Research and Practice, 4,* 318–325.

Youth Sports

American Sport Education Program. (1994). *Sport parent.* Champaign, IL: Human Kinetics.

Burnette, D. (1993). *Youth, sports, and self-esteem: A guide for parents.* Indianapolis: Masters Press.

Fine, A. H., & Sachs, M. L. (1997). *The total sports experience for kids: A parent's guide to success in youth sports.* South Bend, IN: Diamond Communications.

Hogg, J. M. (1997). *Mental skills for young athletes.* Edmonton, AB, Canada: Sport Excel Publishing.

Sports Injuries

Brewer, B., Van Raalte, J., & Linder, D. (1991). Role of the sport psychologist in treating injured athletes. *Journal of Applied Sport Psychology, 3,* 183–190.

Heil, J. (1993). *Psychology of sport injury.* Champaign, IL: Human Kinetics.

Pargman, D. (1993). *Psychological basis of sport injuries.* Morgantown, WV: Fitness Information Technology.

Drug Abuse and Eating Disorders

Thompson, R. A., & Sherman, R. T. (1993). *Helping athletes with eating disorders.* Champaign, IL: Human Kinetics.

Wadler, G., & Hainline, B. (1989). *Drugs and the athlete.* Philadelphia: F. A. Davis Co.

Motor Learning and Exercise Physiology

Brancazio, P. J. (1984). *Sport science: Physical laws and optimum performance.* New York: Simon & Schuster.

Carr, G. (1997). *Mechanics of sport: A practitioner's guide.* Champaign, IL: Human Kinetics.

Christina, R., & Corcos, D. M. (1988). *Coaches guide to teaching sport skills.* Champaign, IL: Human Kinetics.

Sharkey, B. (1986). *Coaches guide to sport physiology.* Champaign, IL: Human Kinetics.

Sharkey, B. J. (1997). *Fitness and health.* Champaign, IL: Human Kinetics.

Practice Development

Granito, V. J., Jr., & Wenz, B. J. (1995). Reading list for professional issues in applied sport psychology. *The Sport Psychologist, 9,* 96–103.

Hays, K. F. (1995). Putting sport psychology into (your) practice. *Professional Psychology: Research and Practice, 26*(1), 33–40.

Hays, K., & Smith, R. (1996). Incorporating sport and exercise psychology into clinical practice. In J. L. Van Raalte & Brewer B. (Eds.), *Exploring sport and exercise psychology* (pp. 413–429). Washington, DC: American Psychological Association.

Petrie, T., & Diehl, N. (1995). Sport psychology in the profession of psychology. *Professional Psychology: Research and Practice, 26,* 288–291.

Simons, J. P., & Anderson, M. B. (1995). The development of consulting practice in applied sport psychology: Some personal perspectives. *The Sport Psychologist, 9,* 449–468.

CONSUMER'S GUIDE TO SPORT PSYCHOLOGY

Betty J. Wenz and Vincent J. Granito, Jr.

What Is Sport Psychology?

Sport psychology is the scientific study of the psychological factors associated with participation and performance in sport, exercise, and other types of physical activity. Sport psychology professionals are interested in two main objectives:

- Performance enhancement through mental training.

- Understanding how participation in sport, exercise, and physical activity affects psychological development, health, and well-being throughout the life span.

What Do You Want from a Sport Psychology Professional?

Carefully determine your needs, and express them to the practitioner as specifically as possible to avoid miscommunication that may prevent obtaining desired results. A sport psychologist can offer a wide variety of services, including: performance enhancement for individuals and/or teams, recovery from injury, treatment of eating disorders, and academic counseling. The professional may focus on specific populations, such as children, the elderly, Olympic trainees, college athletes, professional athletes, or Special Olympians, or on types of problems such as anxiety. For example, someone with a strong background in performance enhancement may be more helpful for increasing concentration skills, combating competition anx-

Note: This consumer's guide is adapted from a soon-to-be published brochure with the generous permission of the authors. It is intended to serve as a guide for individuals interested in utilizing the services of a sport psychology professional.

iety, or maintaining team cohesion. A consultant who is to work with children's groups should have a strong background in child development and psychology as well as sport. An individual coping with personal problems may require a professional with a counseling or therapy background.

Types of Questions to Ask Sport Psychology Professionals

Like consumers of any services, it is wise to be educated as to the types of questions to ask and how to evaluate critically the services provided:

• *What education and experience do you have in sport psychology?* Most university sport psychology training programs are housed in either sport science departments or psychology departments. The practitioner should have at least a master's degree and preferably a doctorate. Ask for a curriculum vita that includes education, how long she or he has worked with athletes, any licensure or certification in sport psychology, membership in relevant professional organizations, and pertinent internship experiences.

• *Do you have experience as a coach, athlete, and/or official? How does that experience affect you as a sport psychology professional?* It is of great value to consult with an individual with experience in athletic competition and/or training who therefore understands some of the psychological demands in sport. *However, the experience as only an ex-athlete, coach, or official does not qualify one to be a sport psychology expert.* Be careful of professionals who use notoriety as coaches or athletes to solicit potential clients.

• *Request a written proposal of the services the professional can provide to meet your needs.* This proposal should respond to your needs as explained in initial conversations. If the proposal reflects the professional's own goals and needs or does not address your or your athletes' requirements, you may refuse the services being offered.

There are other things to look for in a proposal. Can the professional adapt services to any special needs present with your athletes (such as physical disabilities, hearing impairment, athletes with Attention Deficit Hyperactivity Disorder or learning disabilities, or athletes for whom English is a second language)? Does he or she avoid jargon? Educate you about the services he or she will provide?

•   *Do you follow a code of ethics established by a professional organization?*   If the consultant follows a code of ethics, request a copy of this and any other guidelines and procedures that govern his or her practice (such as required reports to legal authorities in the case of suspected child abuse or drug abuse). The code of ethics should include a policy on confidentiality. Request a list of referral sources in the event that services are needed outside the practitioner's scope of practice.

It is considered unethical to guarantee success; however, it is appropriate for a sport psychology professional to state that he or she will apply his or her skills in good faith. Ethics also preclude the practitioner from disclosing the names of individual athletes or teams without permission. However, this person should indicate types of sports and levels of competition in which she or he has experience (e.g., professional soccer team, training with Olympic gymnasts, collegiate softball league). *If a code of ethics is not followed, be very careful about hiring this individual.*

•   *What title do you use?*   A person may use the title "sport psychologist" only if she or he is a licensed psychologist in the state and has appropriate sport psychology experience. It is customary practice to post such licenses on the wall of one's office; in the absence of such, contact the state board of psychology. Other titles used include "sport psychology consultant," "sports counselor," "mental training consultant," and "mental coach." Of course, the professional's title is not as important as specific training and/or experience in sport psychology.

A Final Word

Do not enter into a contract with a professional with whom you do not feel comfortable. Other resources and professionals are available to meet the goals and needs of the athletes.

INTERNET RESOURCES

Sportpsy Mail List

If you have access to the Internet, this is an excellent resource. When you post an e-mail message to the list, it will be sent automatically to approximately one thousand people across the world who subscribe to the list: sport psychologists, students, athletes, coaches, and others. Postings range from serious discussions of ethical issues, case problems, and philosophy to the sometimes trivial and humorous.

Joining the List

To join (subscribe) the list, send an e-mail message to LISTSERV@ VM.TEMPLE.EDU with the following message: SUBSCRIBE SPORTPSY yourname. No subject is necessary.

yourname (in lowercase letters) should be exactly as you prefer to be addressed, and it may include spaces and periods after initials. A short time later the list server will send you confirmation, if you have been successful. If not, you may need to try again. Michael Sachs is the list coordinator, and if all else fails, he will take the time to help you. He may be contacted at the following e-mail address: V5289E@VM.TEMPLE.EDU.

Once you've succeeded in getting onto the list, you will automatically receive a copy of every message posted, usually three to ten per day. If you wish to discontinue or unsubscribe, send a message to LISTSERV@VM.TEMPLE.EDU that reads exactly as follows: SIGNOFF SPORTPSY.

Posting to the List

Posting a message to the list is simple: send an e-mail message to the following address: SPORTPSY@VM.TEMPLE.EDU. Remember that any message so addressed will be automatically sent to all subscribers.

If you wish to reply to a message posted, your software may direct the reply to the list itself, not the person who posted the message. We frequently encounter a message that the author intended to send privately to one person and ended up posting to a thousand subscribers. Needless to say, this could be quite embarrassing. If you wish to respond to the author of a message "off list" (privately), make sure that you use the person's own e-mail address rather than that of the list.

At first many people are somewhat shy and simply "lurk" or read the list messages without posting. However, it's more fun to be a participant when you have a question or have something to share. I have benefited immensely through my participation.

Wide World Web Sites for Sport and Exercise Psychology

Major Associations and Organizations

American Alliance for Health, Physical Education, Recreation and Dance: http://www.aahperd.org/

American College of Sports Medicine: http://www.acsm.org

Association for the Advancement of Applied Sport Psychology: http://spot.colorado.edu/~aaasp/

Division 47 of the American Psychological Association: http://www.psyc.unt.edu/apadiv47/

North American Society for Psychology of Sport and Physical Activity: http://grove/ufl.edu/~naspspa

Note: This list is adapted with permission from *Surfing the Net: Using the Internet for Success*, by Kevin L. Burke, Vincent J. Granito, and Michael L. Sachs, in the *Directory of Graduate Programs in Applied Sport Psychology* (5th ed.), Michael L. Sachs, Kevin L. Burke, and Shawn J. Gomer, Fitness Information Technology, Inc., Morgantown, West Virginia (in press).

Other Associations and Organizations

American Sport Education Program: http://www.asep.com

Coaching Association of Canada: http://www.coach/ca

Human Kinetics Publishers: http://www.humankinetics.com

Michigan State University's Youth Sports Institute: http://www.educ.msu.edu/units/Dept/PEES/ysi/ysihomc.html

National Alliance for Youth Sports: http://www.nays.org

National Association for Girls and Women in Sport: http://www.aahperd.org/nagws/nagws.html

National Association for Sport and Physical Education: http://www.aahperd.org/naspe/naspe.html

Women's Sports Foundation: http://www.lifetimetv.com/wosport

Sport Psychology–Related Sites

Noel Blundell: http://www.golf.com.au/netcoach/library/blundell.html

Ithaca College Health Science and Human Performance Department: http://www.ithaca.edu/Admissions/Schools/HSHP/Majors/Sport_studies.html

The Mental Edge Article: http://www.ultranet.com/~dupcak/mntledge.html

Mind Tools column on sport psychology: http://www.mindtools.com/

John Murray, for articles on the mental side of tennis: http://tennisserver.com

Ohio Center for Sport Psychology: http://www.sportpsych.org

Performance Enhancement: http://www.bubba.ucc/okstate.edu/wellness/athlete.htm

Brent Russell, for sport psychology workshops offered for coaches:
http://www.rohan.sdsu.edu/dept/coachsci/intro.html

Sportpsy Home Page:
http://www.geocities.com/CollegePark/5686/

Sport psychology and golf:
http://www.golfpsych.com/: http://www.golfweb.com/
instruction/cohn/index.html

Sport Psychology information:
http://spot.colorado.edu/~collinsj/

Sport Psychology in Spain:
http://www.ucm.es/OTROS/Psyap/hispania/cruz.htm

Sport Psychology and weight lifting:
http://www.waf.com/weights/randall/htm

Eileen Udry, Ph.D., University of Oregon, home page:
http://darkwing.uoregon.edu/~udryem/EMUd2.html

University of Washington's Husky Sport Psychology Services:
http://www.weber.u.washington.edu/~hsps/

Cristina Versair, *Self-help and Psychology* magazine:
http://www.cybertowers.com/selfhelp/

Other Resources

Explanation of sport science journals, including *Sport Psychology*:
http://www.teach.virginia.edu/curry/resources/library/handouts/
explainsj.html

Internet information on sport psychology:
http://www.gettysburg.edu/response/ref/sportspsy.html

Mental Health Net, Web resource for health and sport psychology:
http://www.cmhc.com/guide/pro07.htm

Psychology of Sport and Exercise link:
http://www.livjm.acuk/sports_science/psycholo.htm

Resource list in both psychology and sport psychology:
http://www.integres.org/prevres/v2n2abst.htm

Research sources for sport psychology:
http://www.server.bmod.athabascau.ca/html/aupr/sport.htm

Specific Sport Information Sites

Amateur Softball Association: http://www.softball.org

American Youth Sport Soccer Organization:
http://www.soccer.org

CNN Sports: http://www.cnn.com/SPORTS/index.html

ESPN's Sport Zone: http://espnet.sportzone.com

Golf: http://www.lgolf.com: http://www.golfweb.com

The Grandstand: http://www.gstand.com

Major League Baseball: http://www.majorleaguebaseball.com

National Basketball Association: http://www.nba.com

National Hockey League: http://www.nhl.com

Olympic Games, Sydney 2000:
http://www.sydney.olympic.org

Parents, children, and sports:
http://www.uvol.com/family/pbseries.html

Sport information: http://www.sportquest.com

Sport Information Resource Center (SIRC): http://sirc.ca/

Sports Illustrated On-Line: http://www.pathfinder.com/si/

Stadiums and arenas: http://www.wwcd.com/stadiums/html

Title IX Information: http://www.arcade.uiowa.edu/proj/ge/

United States Golf Association: http://www.usga.org

United States Swimming: http://www.usswim.org

United States Tennis Association: http://www.usta.com/

USA Hockey: http://www.usahockey.com

USA Today Sports Section:
  http://www.usatoday.com/sports/sfront.htm

USA Wrestling: http://www.usawrestling.org

U.S. Youth Soccer Association: http://www.usysa.org

Winter Paralympics 2002:
  http://www.vsnet.ch/Sion2002/para_e.html

MENTAL SKILLS ASSESSMENT FORM
Ohio Center for Sport Psychology

Name _____ Sport _____ Date _____

Age _____   Sex: Male _____   Female _____

(Please complete this questionnaire without discussing it with anyone.)

1. Below is a list of reasons that people sometimes participate in sports. Please read the list carefully and think of why you participate in your sport. Then:

   a. Place a small check mark on the line in front of the <u>five most important reasons</u> for your participation.

   b. Rank the items that you have checked in order of their importance for you, by placing a number from one to five next to the check mark in front of each of your selections, "one" being the most important reason for your participation, "two" being the next most important reason, and so on.

   ____ a. Becoming a healthier person

   ____ b. Improving my skills

   ____ c. Having fun

   ____ d. Making and enjoying friends

   ____ e. Excitement of competition

   ____ f. Learning social skills

   ____ g. Developing confidence in myself as a person

   ____ h. Winning in competition

   ____ i. Earning respect from other people

   ____ j. Learning life skills: such as setting goals, dealing with frustration, etc.

   ____ k. Earning self-respect

   ____ l. Performing well in competition

   ____ m. Doing something I do well

   ____ n. Being part of a team

   ____ o. Financial gains: salary, scholarships, etc.

2. Place a check mark in front of the five items that you selected on the previous page. Now answer the following questions for each of the five items.

To what extent have you had the following experiences as a result of participating in your sport during the past two weeks? After each item please circle the number that represents your experience. Have you participated in organized competition during this time period?

_____ Y   _____ N

	Not at All				A Great Deal
a. Becoming a healthier person	1	2	3	4	5
b. Improving my skills	1	2	3	4	5
c. Having fun	1	2	3	4	5
d. Making and enjoying friends	1	2	3	4	5
e. Excitement of competition	1	2	3	4	5
f. Learning social skills	1	2	3	4	5
g. Developing confidence in myself as a person	1	2	3	4	5
h. Winning in competition	1	2	3	4	5
i. Earning respect from other people	1	2	3	4	5
j. Learning life skills: such as setting goals, dealing with frustration, etc.	1	2	3	4	5
k. Earning self-respect	1	2	3	4	5
l. Perfoming well in competition	1	2	3	4	5
m. Doing something I do well	1	2	3	4	5
n. Being part of a team	1	2	3	4	5
o. Financial gains: salary, scholarships, etc.	1	2	3	4	5

3. To what extent do you feel a pressure to perform well from each of the following people? Place a circle around the number corresponding to your answer.

	No Pressure at All			A Great Amount of Pressure	
a. Mother	1	2	3	4	5
b. Father	1	2	3	4	5
c. Spouse (or significant other)	1	2	3	4	5
d. Other relatives	1	2	3	4	5
e. Friends	1	2	3	4	5
f. Coach	1	2	3	4	5
g. Teammates	1	2	3	4	5
h. Other competitors	1	2	3	4	5
i. Self	1	2	3	4	5
j. Others (specify) _____	1	2	3	4	5

4. To what extent do you usually feel relaxed or nervous just before you begin to perform in important competition?

Very Relaxed			Very Nervous	
1	2	3	4	5

5. To what extent do you usually feel relaxed or nervous while performing in important competition?

Very Relaxed			Very Nervous	
1	2	3	4	5

6. While performing in important competition, to what extent are you usually able to maintain your concentration?

Easily Distracted			Total Concentration	
1	2	3	4	5

7. If you are sometimes distracted performing in important competition, what kind of things distract you? Check all that apply.

__ my nerves   __ other people

__ bodily feelings   __ sounds

__ my own thoughts   __ visual stimuli

__ Other (please list): _____

8. If you make a mistake while performing in important competition, how quickly are you usually able to recover and perform well?

Not at All			Very Quickly	
1	2	3	4	5

9. When you "talk" to yourself just before important competition, are you primarily positive or negative?

Very Negative			Very Positive	
1	2	3	4	5

10. How often do you imagine yourself performing in competition?

Never			Very Often	
1	2	3	4	5

11. If you do imagine yourself performing in competition, how vivid are your images?

Very Unclear			Very Vivid	
1	2	3	4	5

12. In your images, how well are you performing?

Very Poorly			Very Well	
1	2	3	4	5

13. When you have performed below your expectations or are discouraged or upset about your sport participation, to what extent do you receive emotional support from each of the following people? Place a circle around the number corresponding to your answer.

	No Emotional Support			A Great Amount of Emotional Support	
a. Mother	1	2	3	4	5
b. Father	1	2	3	4	5
c. Spouse (or significant other)	1	2	3	4	5
d. Other relatives	1	2	3	4	5
e. Friends	1	2	3	4	5
f. Coach	1	2	3	4	5
g. Teammates	1	2	3	4	5
h. Other competitors	1	2	3	4	5
i. Self	1	2	3	4	5
j. Others (specify) _____	1	2	3	4	5

14. Please list several athletes in your sport whom you admire. After each name list the qualities of this athlete that you particularly admire or respect.

Athlete   *Qualities*

_____   _____

_____   _____

_____   _____

_____   _____

15. If your sport has an in-season and an off-season, please give the approximate dates for the beginning and end of your in-season.

    In-season begins _____   In-season ends _____

16. Approximately how many hours per week do you spend practicing and competing in your sport?

    In-season hours per week ____   Off-season hours per week ____

17. On the average, to what extent is your life in balance during your in-season? Please express your answer by circling the appropriate number.

In-Season

1	2	3	4	5
Too much time and energy devoted to nonsport activities		Comfortable balance		Too much time and energy devoted to sport

18. On the average, to what extent is your life in balance during your off-season? Please express your answer by circling the appropriate number.

Off-Season

1	2	3	4	5
Too much time and energy devoted to nonsport activities		Comfortable balance		Too much time and energy devoted to sport

About the Author

JACK J. LESYK, PH.D., is a clinical and sport psychologist and the director of the Ohio Center for Sport Psychology, an independent practice organization. Since 1981, he has worked with athletes from over twenty different sports, at competitive levels ranging from scholastic to world-class, Olympic, and professional. He is a clinical adviser to the American Running and Fitness Association, as well as a former contributing editor to *Ohio Runner* magazine, for which he wrote a column on the mental aspects of sport. An avid runner, he has competed in the New York, Chicago, and Boston marathons. In addition to his practice, Dr. Lesyk is an adjunct assistant professor of psychology at Cleveland State University and is listed in the *World Who's Who in Sport Psychology*. A frequent speaker at professional, civic, and social organizations, he is known for his belief that sports should enhance one's overall well-being and joy of living.

Dr. Lesyk can be contacted on the Internet at jjlesyk@sportpsych.org

Index

A

Addiction to exercise, 47–48

Adolescent elite athletes, 145–147. *See also* Young athletes

Advertising: in mass media, 168–171; and professional identity, 159; in sport-specific media, 176. *See also* Marketing; Mass media marketing

Affirmations, positive, 77

Aging athletes: new roles for, 122; recreational, 121–123; women, 113–115

Albee, G., *xv*

American Psychological Association (APA), Division 47, Sport and Exercise Psychology: contact information for, 18; membership in, 27; professional education activities of, 20

Anger: and emotional control techniques, 78–80, 140–141; and young athletes, 106, 140. *See also* Emotional control

Anxiety: arousal control techniques for, 63–68; attention control techniques for, 73–74; avoidance of, 63; imagination and, 64; performance and, 63, 64; prescribed exercise for, 34, 35, 37, 39, 45

Arousal control: assessment and intervention plan for, 138; for clinical clients, 63–68; for committed athletes, 138; optimum arousal level and, 64; for performance enhancement, 10, 63–68; preperformance routine for, 67–68, 138; relaxation training for, 64–67, 138

Assessment: of committed athletes, 135–142; of injured athletes, 119; intake, 98–99, 135–136; for mental skills intervention planning, 136–142; for possible psychological problems, 135–136; of recreational athletes, 98–99, 104, 119; of sport motivation and satisfaction, 98–99; of young athletes, 104. *See also* Mental Skills Assessment Form

Association for the Advancement of Applied Sport Psychology (AAASP): Certified Consultant program, 26–28; contact information for, 19; ethical guidelines of, 29; journal of, 17; meetings of, 20; membership directory of, 21; professional education activities of, 20, 23–24

Associations: coaches', 173–174; sport psychologist, 18–20, 189

Athletes: aging, 121–123; casual participant, 87–88; categories of, 86–90; as clients, 90–96; committed, 89–90, 125–142; confidentiality

45, 46; maintenance of, 38, 44–45; minimum time requirements for, 34; psychological benefits of, 32–33, 45, 49, 181–182; psychological risks of, 47–48; readings about, 181–182, 183; relationship improvements from, 49–51; requirements of, for psychological benefit, 34; self-monitoring for, 45; therapist roles in, 45–46; types of, 34, 40

Expert approach, to sport psychology practice, 155–156

Experts: sport psychology, 130–131; sports-specific, 128–129. *See also* Mentoring

F

Fairness/unfairness, and young athletes, 107

Family conflict/dysfunction: and women athletes, 110–112, 117, 118–119; and young athletes, 104–105, 145, 151; and young elite athletes, 144. *See also* Parents

Fear of flying: mental rehearsal script for, in case example, 81–83; sport psychology techniques for, in case example, 53–54. *See also* Anxiety

Figure skating, *xx–xxii*; adolescents in, 146; organizational structure of, 172; videotapes of, 130; vocabulary of, 130

Financial issues: evaluation of, 5; office location and, 3–4

Focus control. *See* Attention control

Focused marketing, 166–167, 171–178; to coaches, 173–174; direct mail for, 176; organizational structure of target sport and, 172; presentations for, 174–175; selecting a target sport for, 132–133, 172; at sporting events, 176; sport-specific media and, 176

Football player, college, 131

G

Galvanic skin response (GSR) monitoring, 66

Goal setting: assessment and intervention plan for, 137; in case example, 61–63; for clinical clients, 59–63; for committed athletes, sport-related, 137; for committed athletes, therapeutic, 136; for exercise program, 40–43; for mental skills training, 136; motivation clarification and, 58–59; for performance enhancement, 10, 59–63; for sports psychology practice, 156–157

Golf: attention control and, 71; mental skills readings about, 180–181; recreational, 88, 89

Golfer, working with, in case scenario, 133–142

Granito, V., Jr., 21, 184

Group dynamics, 12

Guided imagery, relaxation and, 66–67. *See also* Mental imagery techniques; Relaxation training

Gymnastics, videotapes of, 130

H

Handouts: and professional identity, 159; topical, 161

Harris, D., *xx, xxiii*

Hays, K. F., 45–46, 51

Hoop Dreams, 147

Hypnosis, *xx, xxi*; for relaxation training, 66

I

Imagery. *See* Guided imagery; Mental imagery, 66

Infinity volleyball, 102

Information resources: experts as, 128–129; Internet, 23–25, 131, 188–193; reading, 17–18, 130, 179–183; television and videotape, 129–130. *See also* Internet resources; Professional development; Readings

Stationery, and professional identity,
159
Stock advertisements, 161
Stress management: exercise and,
34, 37; programs for, *xvi–xvii*
Substance abuse treatment, 55;
readings about, 183. *See also*
Addiction to exercise; Eating
disorders; Smoking cessation
Suinn, R., *xx, xxiii*

T
Talk shows, 169–170, 171
Targeted marketing. *See* Focused
marketing
Team building, 12
Team consultation, 11–12, 158
Telephone answering, 164
Television advertising, interview and
talk show, 169–171
Television watching, for gaining
sports-specific knowledge, 129–130
Testimonials, for marketing, 162
Therapist. *See* Clinician
Title IX, Education Amendments
Act, 112
Treatment modalities, assessment of,
in clinical practice, 4
Trigger word/phrase, for relaxa-
tion, 66, 67, 78. *See also* Cue
word/phrase

U
U.S. Department of Health and
Human Services, 32, 51
U.S. Olympic Committee: Advisory
Board on Sport Psychology, 7;
first sport psychology conference,
xxii–xxiii; Sport Psychology Reg-
istry, 21, 27

V
Videotapes, for gaining sports-specific
knowledge, 129–130
Vocabulary, sports-specific, 130

W
Waitley, D., *xxiii*
Walking, 40
Wealth, of professional athletes, 149,
150
Weight control: exercise and, 34, 35,
37; programs, *xvi–xvii*
Wenz, B. J., *xxiii*, 21, 184
White, R. W., *xv, xxiv*
Whole person, balanced with sport,
97–99, 126, 135, 144
Wolpe, J., 54
Women athletes, recreational,
110–119; assertiveness and, 118;
case examples of, 110–112,
113–114, 115–117, 118–119;
conflicts of, 110–112, 117–119;
elderly, 113–115; family conflict
and, 110–112, 117–119; middle-
generation, 116–119; and social
change, 112, 114–115, 116; young,
115–116
Work satisfaction, clinician, *xiv, xvi,
xxiv*, 157
Workshops: for marketing, 171,
177–178; for professional education, 20–21; as service to offer, 158,
177–178. *See also* Educational sport
psychology
World Wide Web, 24–25; clinician
home pages on, 25; sport psychology sites on, 24, 189–192; sport-
specific sites on, 131, 192–193.
See also Internet
Wrestler, adolescent, 145–146

Y
Yellow Pages, 169
Young athletes, 90; accepting criticism and, 107–108; anger and,
106, 140; case example of, 99–
100, 108–109; cognitive restructuring for, 106–109; communication of, 106–107; conflicts of,
99–100, 101; counseling, 102–109;